The Gospel of John

Life through Believing

SURVEY OF THE SCRIPTURES
BASIC BIBLE COMMENTARY

The Gospel of John

Life through Believing

Dr. Alfred Martin

MERIDIAN
PUBLICATIONS

Contents

Preface

To begin to understand the specifics of in-depth Bible study, we need a picture of how the entire Bible fits together.

The *Survey of the Scriptures* series is a tour through the Bible that points out how one section relates to another, each subject to the whole. By knowing how each part relates to the others, we can better appreciate and apply its lessons. Then the series concentrates on individual books of the Bible.

Meridian titles in addition to *John—Life through Believing* in the *Survey of the Scriptures* currently include:

The New Testament—Matthew through Revelation

Matthew—Gospel of the King

Acts—Power for Witnessing

Romans—Amazing Grace

Revelation—God's Final Word to Man

Additional titles in the *Survey of the Scripture* series are forthcoming.

For many years Dr. Alfred Martin taught these *Survey of the Scriptures* as "Bible 101" at Moody Bible Institute and later at Dallas Bible Institute and at Southern Bible Institute. For over thirty years the summary of his work has been published as a Bible correspondence course for the External Studies Division of Moody Bible Institute.

Now for the first time this incisive and insightful study of John is available for personal or group Bible study, providing a more in-depth look at the book than the general surveys in the *Survey of the Scriptures* series.

Thirty years ago I graduated from Moody Bible Institute with a foundation in God's Word built on *Survey of the Scriptures*. As Dr. Martin then opened up the Bible to a new understanding and appreciation to me, I now am proud to be able to publish his survey materials so that you too can better appreciate how each portion of God's Word fits into the whole.

—The Publisher

*I*ntroduction

To see the Bible as a whole is not only vital to a proper understanding of the Bible; it is also a thrilling experience!

Survey of the Scriptures, first written as a Bible study course by Dr. Alfred Martin, Vice President and Dean of Education Emeritus of Moody Bible Institute, Chicago, is based in part on a former course by Dr. James M. Gray, past president of Moody Bible Institute. Dr. Martin quotes Dr. Gray throughout the *Survey*. Maps and charts were prepared by John Phillips, author of the several Exploring the Scriptures titles. John Phillips was director of both Moody and Emmaus correspondence schools.

In addition to the general *Survey* books, this book and others provide study material on individual books of the Bible for a closer look at specific areas of Scripture.

The Gospel of John was written "so that you might believe that Jesus is the Christ, the Son of God; and that believing you might have life through his name" (John 20:30–31).

This commentary, rather than being a complete study of the gospel of John, is an introduction to get you started on a lifetime of Bible study and Christian growth.

Because these materials were initially used both as classroom and correspondence school texts, Dr. Martin's style is one of a teacher—guiding, challenging, directing, stimulating, and raising questions as well as providing answers.

Various ways of studying the Bible are suggested for further study. And each section concludes with a daily devotional reading plan so that the book can also be used as a quarterly reading guide or for Bible study.

The content of this edition is taken from an adult credit course from Moody Bible Institute, External Studies Division. For information on how you might take this and other courses for credit, write for a free catalog to:

Moody External Studies
Moody Bible Institute
820 N. La Salle
Chicago, IL 60610

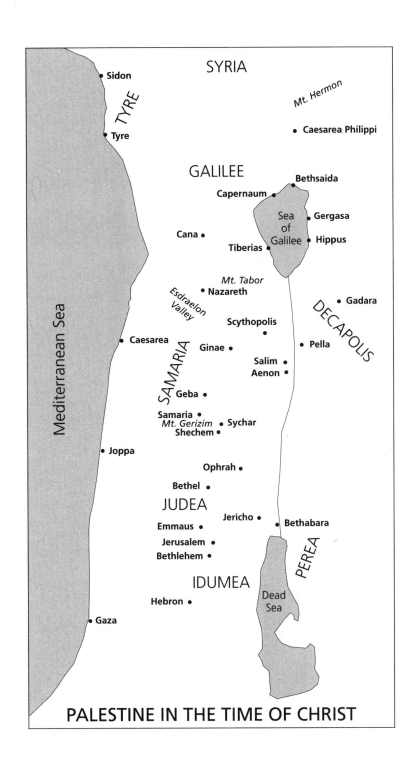

PALESTINE IN THE TIME OF CHRIST

The Most Useful Book in the World

"These [signs] are written that you might believe" (20:31).

Our aim in this first chapter is to get a general impression of the Gospel of John, including its purpose, its specific emphasis, its basic structure, its "signposts."

THE PURPOSE OF JOHN

This particular book of the Bible, the Gospel according to John, was especially designed by God for the most wonderful and useful purpose: to tell people about the Lord Jesus Christ, the Son of God, so that they might believe in him and thereby receive eternal life. This is not supposition, for the book itself gives this as its purpose:

And many other signs truly did Jesus in the presence of his disciples, which are not written in this book: but these are written, that you might believe that Jesus is the Christ, the Son of God; and that believing you might have life through his name (John 20:30–31).

NOT A COMPLETE BIOGRAPHY

These words indicate that it was not the writer's intention to write a complete biography of the Lord Jesus Christ. Under the guidance of the Holy Spirit he chose events in the Lord's earthly life and ministry that show that he is the promised Savior and the Son of God.

God has given us four records of the earthly life of his Son. These accounts—we commonly call them the four Gospels—supplement one another. No one book pretends to tell everything about the Lord Jesus. In fact we are told in this one that a complete story would be impossible:

> And there are also many other things which Jesus did, which, if they should be written every one, I suppose that even the world itself could not contain the books that should be written (John 21:25).

DIFFERENT EMPHASIS IN EACH GOSPEL

Each of the Gospel records has a particular emphasis.

Matthew presents Jesus Christ as the *King*.

Mark presents him as the *Servant*.

Luke presents him as the perfect *Man*.

John presents him as *God*.

We would be making a great mistake, however, if we thought that only one of these four aspects of Christ's Person and work is set forth in each Gospel. He is all of these in all of them. The emphasis is the thing to watch in each book.

14

THE WRITER

The Gospel of John was the last of the four to be written. The writer assumes that many of his readers already know the things that have been written in the other accounts. He omits almost entirely the ministry of the Lord Jesus in Galilee (although he does include distinctive miracles performed there—the turning of water into wine at Cana and the healing of the nobleman's son). He concentrates on the Lord's ministry in Jerusalem and in other parts of the province of Judea.

It is fitting that the one who had an intimate knowledge of the events should have been chosen by God to write this account. The writer is undoubtedly John, the son of Zebedee, who never refers to himself by name in the book. He prefers to call himself the "disciple whom Jesus loved" (John 13:23; 19:26; 20:2; 21:7, 20, 24), not claiming by the use of the title a place of superiority over the other apostles, but delighting to testify that the love of the Lord Jesus is a personal love toward each individual, and that it included him too.

STRUCTURE OF THE BOOK

You must not think of this commentary as a complete study of the Gospel of John. This book, so simple and clear on the surface, has defied analysis by great and devout scholars. It is profound; it is inexhaustible. What you will find here is an introduction to a lifetime of study and enjoyment of this record of our Lord by the disciple he loved.

A simple working outline divides the book into two main parts:

CHRIST'S MINISTRY TO THE WORLD (chapters 1–12)

CHRIST'S MINISTRY TO HIS OWN (chapters 13–21)

A somewhat more exact division would be:

PROLOGUE: THE ETERNAL WORD (1:1–18)

CHRIST'S MINISTRY TO THE WORLD (1:19–12:50)

CHRIST'S MINISTRY TO HIS OWN (13:1–17:26)

CHRIST'S DEATH AND RESURRECTION (18:1–20:31)

EPILOGUE: THE RISEN LORD (21:1–25)

DISTINCTIVE FEATURES OF THE BOOK

There are a number of signs in the gospel of John. Also, as you read and reread the book, you will become aware of key words that help to open up the meaning of a passage. Several of these words are especially significant. They will not be mentioned at this time, but you should try to discover what they are.

John stresses the "signs" or miracles (20:30–31) and describes seven outstanding miracles in the first major division of the book:

1. Turning of water into wine (chapter 2)

2. Healing of the nobleman's son (chapter 4)

3. Healing of the helpless man (chapter 5)

4. Feeding of the five thousand (chapter 6)

5. Walking on the water (chapter 6)

6. Healing of a man born blind (chapter 9)

7. Raising of Lazarus from the dead (chapter 11)

In view of the announced purpose of the writer (20:30–31), which we have already noted, we can see that these "signs" are basic to the understanding of the book. They all show that Jesus is the Christ, the Son of God.

In addition to the seven signs, there are seven distinct statements of the Lord Jesus that begin with "I AM" and end with a descriptive title:

1. "I AM the Bread of Life" (6:35).

2. "I AM the Light of the World" (8:12).

3. "I AM the Door" (10:9).

4. "I AM the Good Shepherd" (10:11).

5. "I AM the Resurrection and the Life" (11:25).

6. "I AM the Way, the Truth, and the Life" (14:6).

7. "I AM the True Vine" (15:1).

Key words, signs, and "I AM" sayings are characteristics of the gospel of John that make it distinctive. Another distinctive is its personal interviews between the Lord Jesus and various individuals in different walks of life. The two that are featured in the early part of the book are with Nicodemus, a respected Jewish teacher (chapter 3), and with the Samaritan woman (chapter 4). Others are:

with the nobleman whose son was seriously ill (chapter 4)
with the former blind man (chapter 9)
with Martha of Bethany (chapter 11)
and with her sister Mary (chapter 11).

In addition to the personal interviews, there are discourses to the multitude and to the disciples. Some of these arise from the miracles. The best known and longest is the "upper-room discourse" (beginning in chapter 13).

John gives more space than any of the other Gospels to the last week of our Lord's ministry before the crucifixion and resurrection. Almost half of this Gospel is devoted to that brief period.

Here it is in all its panoramic glory—this most useful of all books. By God's grace discover at the outset that its usefulness is in the Person whom it presents, the Lord Jesus Christ, and determine to appropriate this usefulness for yourself.

God's purpose for you is that you "might believe that Jesus is the Christ, the Son of God" (20:31). Do you believe this?

2

The Eternal Word Among Men

"These things were done . . . beyond
Jordan, where John was baptizing"
(1:28).

John 1–2

STUDY SUGGESTIONS

From time to time various ways of studying the gospel of
John will be suggested even though all the ways cannot be
pursued in this brief book. You may want to study more on
your own.

One method of study, *geographical*, notes the different
localities where the action occurs. In this chapter, for example, we see Bethabara beyond Jordan (1:28), Cana of Galilee
(2:1), and Jerusalem (2:13). See the map on page 11.

Another method, *chronological*, observes the time references in the book. For example, the Passover is mentioned
in 2:13. From the different references to the Passover and

other Jewish feasts, we can reach a conclusion concerning the length of our Lord's ministry.

CONTENTS

While we are not attempting in this study to build an analytical outline of John, we can easily discern five parts (or scenes) in the action of these chapters.

1. THE PROLOGUE—THE WORD MADE FLESH 1:1–18

2. THE RECORD OF JOHN 1:19–34

3. EARLIEST DISCIPLES 1:35–51

4. THE WEDDING AT CANA—THE FIRST SIGN 2:1–11

5. AT JERUSALEM FOR THE PASSOVER 2:12–25

THE WORD MADE FLESH

The opening verses of John are usually called the *Prologue* (1:1–18). Thoughts which are introduced here are developed throughout the book.

At the outset an unusual title confronts us. A person is called "the Word." What does that mean?

A word is the expression of an idea. When the Scripture calls this person the Word, it is emphasizing that he is the expression of God; he is the one who makes God known to men (1:18). Various other titles are used for him. After being introduced as "the Word" (1:1), he is called the "Light" (1:8–9), the "only begotten of the Father" (1:14), and the "only begotten Son" (1:18). Furthermore he is definitely identified as "Jesus Christ" (1:17).

Some of the deepest teachings concerning the person of Christ are found in these verses. His deity is affirmed (1:1). As God, he always existed (1:1–2), is the creator of all things (1:3), and is the source of all life (1:4).

The truth known as the *incarnation* is described in 1:14. Along with the deity of Jesus Christ ("the Word was God") stands the clear proclamation of his true and perfect humanity ("the Word became flesh"). The eternal Son of God became a human being and lived in this world; hence he is the God-Man.

JOHN'S PURPOSE AND THE USE OF KEY WORDS

Everything in the account contributes to the purpose as expressed in John 20:30–31. John's use of key words emphasizes one with the author's singleness of purpose. In the Prologue some of the key words are *life, light, believe*, and *truth*. These and a number of others keep appearing in the Gospel.

What are the two most significant key words in the purpose of the book? Using an inexpensive copy of the gospel of John, underline key words with pencils of different colors. Start out with the four key words mentioned above, and you will discover new ideas opening up to you.

A RECURRING THEME—REJECTION AND RECEPTION

The Prologue is the book in miniature. Verses 10–13 trace the fact and the effects of the life and ministry of the Lord Jesus upon this earth:

> He was in the world, and the world was made by him, and the world knew him not. He came unto his own, and his own

21

received him not. But as many as received him, to them gave he power to become the sons of God, *even* to them that believe on his name: which were born, not of blood, nor of the will of the flesh, nor of the will of man, but of God.

At the very beginning we see how wonderfully the Holy Spirit is working out the stated aim of the book—that men may believe on Jesus Christ, and believing may have life. As you go through the Gospel, you will find these opposite reactions to the Lord Jesus among various individuals and groups—rejection and reception, belief and unbelief.

THE RECORD OF JOHN

The John mentioned here is not the writer. He is introduced in the Prologue (1:6, 15) and named again in 1:19, 26, 29, and 32. He is John the Baptist (Baptizer), whose history is given more fully in the other Gospels, particularly in Luke. Here we see him nobly performing his office as the forerunner of Christ, appointed by God and prophesied in the Old Testament (see Isaiah 40:3; Malachi 3:1). His testimony is without hesitation and without uncertainty. Note the finality of his denials:

And he confessed, and denied not; but confessed, "I am not the Christ." And they asked him, "What then? Are you Elias [Elijah]?" And he said, "I am not. Are you that prophet? And he answered, No!" (1:20–21).

Some men in similar circumstances would have been tempted to claim honors for themselves.

Note the directness, but also the modesty, of his affirmation: "I am the voice of one crying in the wilderness. . . ." He pointed to Isaiah's prophecy, which these religious leaders should have known (Isaiah 40:3). His responsibility was to bear record and he discharged it admirably (see 1:7–8, 15, 19, 32, 34). We have much to learn from John about being faithful witnesses for Jesus Christ!

THE LAMB OF GOD

John's proclamation of Jesus as the "Lamb of God" (1:29) points back to the Old Testament sacrifices and points forward to the cross (compare Isaiah 53:7; 1 Corinthians 5:7; 1 Peter 1:18–20).

This account does not tell of the actual baptism of the Lord Jesus (for that see Matthew 3:13–17; Mark 1:9–11; Luke 3:21–22), but gives John the Baptist's reminiscence of the event. The order of the narrative, with its reference to specific days (1:29, 35), seems to indicate that the temptation of the Lord Jesus, described in Matthew 4:1–11 and Luke 4:1–13, had taken place between the time of his baptism and the day on which John the Baptist proclaimed him to be the "Lamb of God" (1:29).

EARLIEST DISCIPLES

Those interested in related questions might well ask about the connection between the events recorded in John 1:35–51 and the calling of the disciples to service (compare Mark 1:16–20). This event in John is obviously the earlier one.

If one of these first disciples was Andrew, who was the other? Probably John, the writer. What time of day was it when these two visited Jesus (1:39)? This is not as simple as it sounds. Later time references in the Gospel will be alluded to in other sections.

These early disciples came to Christ in different ways. We can see, though, that the most common was through the testimony of someone else, the invitation of a friend or relative. Andrew brought Peter; Philip brought Nathanael; someone probably brought you. Whom have you brought?

WATER CHANGED TO WINE—THE FIRST SIGN

The Lord Jesus socialized. On the occasion described here he was attending a wedding (2:1–11).

The words spoken by the Lord Jesus to his mother (2:4) probably did not sound so severe in the original as they do in our English translation, but they do put us on our guard against any undue exaltation of Mary. Her attitude was exemplary, and her words could serve as a motto for every one of us: "Whatever he says to you, do it" (2:5).

In the miracle which he performed, the Lord Jesus showed himself to have transforming power over nature. He "manifested forth his glory" (2:11).

Remember the purpose of the book: "These [signs] are written, that you might believe that Jesus is the Christ, the Son of God. . . ."

AT JERUSALEM FOR THE PASSOVER

After the brief mention of our Lord's stay in Capernaum (2:12), his visit to Jerusalem for the Passover is described. Much of the action in this gospel takes place in Jerusalem at the time of various sacred observances.

Confusion in Bible study comes from identifying similar events as one and the same. The cleansing of the temple described here (2:14–17) is certainly not the same event as the one described in the other gospels (Matthew 21:12–13; Mark 11:15–17; Luke 19:45–46). This is early in Christ's ministry; that in the other gospels was toward its close. In this he accuses the people of making the temple "a house of merchandise"; in that, a "den of robbers."

When asked for a sign, the Lord Jesus answered cryptically (as he often did to those who asked hostile questions), but the later events opened the eyes of his disciples to his meaning (2:22).

Different kinds of belief are indicated in various places in this Gospel. Apparently the belief of many (described in 2:23) was only a superficial acquiescence in what they saw, not the true belief of wholehearted acceptance (1:12).

PERSONAL APPLICATION

As you think of the attitude of the disciples after the first miracle (2:11), and the attitude of the crowd in Jerusalem when they saw his miracles there (2:23), ask yourself which characterizes your own belief? Is yours the belief of mental assent to truth alone, or have you experienced the belief of personal and complete acceptance of the Lord Jesus Christ?

DAILY DEVOTIONAL READINGS

As you read each passage, look for: (1) An example to follow; (2) A command to obey; (3) A promise to claim; (4) A warning to note; (5) A prayer to use; (6) The main lesson; (7) A best verse to memorize; and (8) Something new about the Christian life.

Sunday
John 1:1–18
God with us

Monday
John 1:19–28
John the forerunner

Tuesday
John 1:29–34
John's witness to Jesus

Wednesday
John 1:35–42
The first followers

Thursday
John 1:43–51
Philip, Nathanael and Jesus

Friday
John 2:1–11
Water into wine at a wedding

Saturday
John 2:12–25
Jesus in Jerusalem

3

Two Momentous Interviews

"And he had to pass through Samaria . . ." (4:4 NASB).

John 3–4

CONTENTS

There are four main sections in these chapters, two of which we will emphasize in this lesson.

1. THE INTERVIEW WITH NICODEMUS—THE NEW BIRTH (3:1–21)

2. THE FRIENDS OF THE BRIDEGROOM (3:22–36)

3. THE INTERVIEW WITH THE SAMARITAN WOMAN—THE WATER OF LIFE (4:1–42)

4. THE HEALING OF THE NOBLEMAN'S SON—THE
   SECOND SIGN (4:43–54)

THE INTERVIEW WITH NICODEMUS—
THE NEW BIRTH

Jesus talked to two very different people in John 3 and 4, yet their basic problem was the same. The Jewish religious leader and the immoral Samaritan woman both needed the Savior.

It is impossible to determine precisely why Nicodemus came to Jesus at night (3:1–2). His visit was prompted by the miracles that the Lord Jesus had performed during his visit in Jerusalem (compare 2:23 and 3:2). Rather than condemn him for his timidity, or even cowardice, we should commend him for coming. He is mentioned twice more in the Gospel (7:50 and 19:39).

There is no record that Nicodemus asked a question at the beginning of the interview. He opened with a statement of his belief that Jesus came from God (3:2). However, the Lord Jesus, who knows men's hearts (2:25), answered the question that Nicodemus really wanted to ask (3:3).

The teaching of the Lord Jesus concerning the new birth has already been anticipated in the Prologue (1:12–13). Although Nicodemus professed bewilderment, there is indication that he could, and probably should, have known this truth from his acquaintance with the Old Testament (3:10).

The central passage the Lord Jesus had in mind may have been from Ezekiel:

> Then I will sprinkle clean water on you, and you shall be clean; I will cleanse you from all your filthiness and from all your idols. I will give you a new heart and put a new spirit within you; I will take the heart of stone out of your flesh

and give you a heart of flesh. I will put My Spirit within you and cause you to walk in My statutes, and you will keep My judgments and do them (Ezekiel 36:25–27 NKJV).

Natural birth and position cannot give a person a right standing before God. There must be an entirely new relationship—a birth from above (compare 2 Corinthians 5:17; 1 Peter 1:23; 1 John 5:1; Titus 3:4–7). This supernatural work of the Holy Spirit of God (3:8) takes place when a person exercises personal faith in the Lord Jesus Christ.

To show the condition that must be fulfilled on the human side, the Lord Jesus cited an illustration from the Old Testament (3:14). The historical record of the brazen serpent in the wilderness (Numbers 21:4–9), with which Nicodemus would be familiar, was used to show the element of faith—that is, true belief. The Israelite who had been bitten was told that if he looked toward the serpent of brass he would be healed. Real faith takes God at his word and does just what he asks.

In this well-known passage of John we find two familiar key words—*believe* and *life.* The two always go together. There can be no eternal life apart from a personal relationship to Jesus Christ, the Son of God. The most familiar of all Bible verses states this plainly:

> For God so loved the world that He gave His only begotten Son, that whoever believes in Him should not perish but have everlasting life (3:16 NKJV).

THE FRIEND OF THE BRIDEGROOM

Again we are permitted a glimpse of the Lord's noble forerunner, who here characterizes himself as the "friend of the bridegroom" (3:29) who rejoices in his joy. John in his renunciation of self and his glorification of Christ is a pattern for every true believer: "He must increase, but I must decrease" (3:30).

All people *must* be born again in order to see and enter into the kingdom of God (3:3, 5, 7). Christ *must* be lifted up (3:14) to die as a sacrifice for the sins of the world. Christ *must* increase (3:30). These are divine imperatives.

THE INTERVIEW WITH THE SAMARITAN WOMAN—THE WATER OF LIFE

The Lord Jesus often used things in the natural world to illustrate spiritual truth. With Nicodemus he used the wind (3:8). With the Samaritan woman he used a drink of water (4:7).

The woman was astonished that he should ask her for a drink (4:9), and further perplexed as she heard him say:

> "If you knew the gift of God, and who it is who says to you, 'Give Me a drink,' you would have asked Him, and He would have given you living water" (4:10 NKJV).

With incredulity—and perhaps with sarcasm—she referred to his lack of means to draw water and compared him to Jacob, whom she claimed as her ancestor. This was the occasion for a promise from the Lord Jesus of lasting satisfaction. He pointed out the natural law. There was nothing wrong with the water in the well, but it could not satisfy thirst permanently. This is the inherent characteristic of earthly things in general, even of things that are good in themselves.

The "water" that the Lord Jesus promised is different. Certain things can be noticed about it:

1. It is a gift from Christ himself (4:14).

Although water is sometimes used in Scripture as a symbol of the Holy Spirit (as in John 7:37–39), and sometimes as a symbol of the Word of God (as in Ephesians 5:26), it seems here to signify salvation with all the benefits that accompany it (compare Isaiah 12:3). The last invitation in the Bible proclaims the same gospel call: "Let him that is thirsty come. And whoever will, let him take the water of life freely" (Revelation 22:17).

The Bible repeats over and over again the glorious fact that salvation is a gift (compare this passage with Ephesians 2:8–9 and Romans 6:23).

2. One drink will satisfy forever (4:14).

This is shown by the tense of the verb in the original language. The sentence might be translated as follows:

> But whoever drinks of the water that I shall give him will never thirst (4:14 NKJV).

This follows from the very nature of the spiritual water. The thirst of the body must be satisfied from without. The soul that has drunk the water of life never thirsts because that water keeps springing up within.

Satisfaction! The world is seeking it, but does not know its meaning. Satisfaction can come only by accepting the gift of God. Does it last?

Yes. The text declares it, and experience confirms it. The Christian life becomes richer and fuller as time goes on (compare Proverbs 4:18).

3. It can be received through believing (4:15).

There is no way of knowing positively what was in the heart of the Samaritan woman as she asked for this water, but even though she did not understand the Lord Jesus' words, and even if she spoke jestingly, she did have a longing for something better than the transitory things of her experience.

Her condition was exactly like that of everyone who does not know the Lord Jesus Christ. The world may put on its best smile and exhibit its brightest manner, but it cannot get rid of the aching heart underneath.

Christ offers something that will absolutely satisfy every longing of the human heart; in fact, he himself is that satisfaction. This is the same gospel that the Lord gave to Nicodemus, even though it is expressed differently.

Through the death of the Lord Jesus Christ on Calvary, God can and does offer eternal life to anyone who believes.

4. This truth has an application to believers.

Many Christians are living in such a way that they can hardly be distinguished from the people of the world.

They are still trying to quench their spiritual thirst by gulping down great draughts of the water of the world. How foolish!

Like Israel of old, such Christians have "committed two evils":

> They have forsaken me [the Lord] the fountain of living waters, and hewed them out cisterns, broken cisterns, that can hold no water (Jeremiah 2:13).

Yet in spite of our failure, the words of the Lord Jesus are still true; and our hearts—even when cold—must answer, "Amen." The only qualification needed to come to Christ is thirst—to know a longing, burning thirst that seems unquenchable.

Whatever your need—whether it is salvation or deeper spiritual fellowship—you may come, you can come, you should come to Jesus Christ and drink.

It was to the Samaritan woman that the Lord Jesus gave the wonderful teaching that God who is a Spirit must be worshiped in spirit and in truth (4:24). Among the Samaritans he was given a title that described the universality of his mission—"the Savior of the world" (4:42).

HEALING OF THE NOBLEMAN'S SON—THE SECOND SIGN

In Cana of Galilee, where Jesus performed his first miracle, he demonstrated his divine power once again, this time over human illness. At Christ's word the sick boy in Capernaum recovered. In these signs the Lord Jesus is showing that he is the Christ, the Son of God. Here he demonstrates his claim to be the One who said to his people in the Old Testament, "I am the Lord who heals you" (Exodus 15:26 NKJV).

Note the growing faith of the nobleman (4:50, 53). This is not blind faith, but belief based upon the knowledge that the object of faith is completely trustworthy.

FOR EXTRA STUDY

1. Trace the journeys of the Lord Jesus on the map. The Scripture says, "He must go through Samaria" (4:4). This would seem at first to be a geographical necessity since Samaria was between Judea and Galilee. Because of their racial prejudice, however, the Jews customarily did not go through Samaria, but crossed and recrossed the Jordan River in their travels between the northern and southern provinces. This *must* is, therefore, an inner compulsion in the heart of the Lord Jesus rather than a geographical necessity.

2. Study the origin of the Samaritans and their worship on Mount Gerizim—"this mountain" (4:20)—with the aid of a Bible dictionary or Bible encyclopedia. Their origin is given in 2 Kings 17:24–41.

3. Consider the question in connection with an earlier reference to 1:39: What time of day was it when the Samari-

tan woman came to the well (4:6)? These are not the only references to the time of day in the Gospel (compare 4:52). Later passages will help you answer this question.

These are added suggestions for fascinating lines of study that can be followed in John. But in taking any of these paths, always remember the main trail—the way of *life* through *belief* in the person and work of the Son of God.

DAILY DEVOTIONAL READINGS

Sunday
John 3:1–8
The new birth

Monday
John 3:9–21
Salvation in the Son

Tuesday
John 3:22–36
John—the Bridegroom's friend

Wednesday
John 4:1–14
Two wells of water

Thursday
John 4:15–30
Christ—the soul-winner

Friday
John 4:31–42
Sowing and reaping

Saturday
John 4:43–54
A prayer heard and a son healed

4

Christ
Satisfying Needs

"When the people therefore saw
that Jesus was not there, nor His disciples, they also got into boats and
came to Capernaum, seeking Jesus"
(6:24 NKJV).

John 5–6

THE HEALING OF THE HELPLESS MAN—
THE THIRD SIGN

Most of the action in the Gospel of John takes place in
Jerusalem. As chapter 5 opens, the Lord Jesus goes again to
Jerusalem for "a feast of the Jews" (5:1).

Much has been written about the identity of this feast, but
nothing that is written can be more than speculation. If it was
a Passover, as many believe, then a year would have passed
since the visit described in 2:13. Accordingly, the length of
the Lord's earthly ministry would be established as some-

what over three years, since two other Passover feasts are mentioned in John (6:4 and 12:1).

This third miracle, or sign, in the gospel of John again shows the power of the Lord Jesus to heal. This time a man who had been helpless for thirty-eight years (5:5).

The subsequent objections and persecution arose from the fact that he did the miracle on the Sabbath day (5:9–10, 16).

EQUAL HONOR TO THE SON

The controversy over the healing on the Sabbath soon took on a more serious aspect when the Lord Jesus used the miracle as the basis for the teaching concerning his deity. Asserting that his Father works unceasingly, he indicated that he also must pursue his work.

The implications were clear to his original hearers, even if some people today profess to find the teaching obscure. One implication is that God's rest after the creation was broken by man's sin, and that ever since God has been engaged in the ceaseless work of redemption.

The more obvious inference, which the Jews grasped immediately, was the claim of the Lord Jesus to be equal with the Father (5:18).

Throughout the Gospel we are confronted with these claims of the Lord Jesus, claims which cannot be ignored. We can trace the mounting tension in the book, the development of the conflict between truth and error, light and darkness, belief and unbelief. At this point the enemies of Christ were determined to kill him (5:16, 18).

Strange to say, they were more consistent in their furious hatred of the Lord than are people today who profess to accept the teachings of Jesus while rejecting the truth concerning who he is. Only the spiritual blindness of unbelief could cause man to reach such false conclusions.

The logic is clear. Either the Lord Jesus was good or he was not good. Most will admit that he was a good man. But he claimed to be God and demanded that all men should honor him exactly as they honor the Father (5:23).

If he were not God, and therefore not deserving of this honor, then his claim would be preposterous and blasphemous, and he would not be a good man. If he is what he claimed to be, then how can anyone refuse to accept him?

In this discourse the Lord Jesus mentions his ability to raise the dead, and his right to be the judge of all men (5:21–22).

Salvation, as always in Scripture, is stated as a fact to be acknowledged by faith, not a mere wish or probability:

> Most assuredly, I say to you, he who hears My word and believes in Him who sent Me has everlasting life, and shall not come into judgment, but has passed from death into life (5:24 NKJV).

WITNESSES TO CHRIST

In the statement of 5:31, the Lord Jesus is not denying the truth of his own witness; he is making a concession to his enemies, who would be quick to assert that he must have independent witnesses to support his claims (compare 8:13). He calls up his witnesses, so to speak.

The first witness is John the Baptizer (5:33). The people generally acknowledged that John was a prophet from God (see Matthew 21:26). His testimony concerning the Lord Jesus was clear enough for all to believe.

The second witness is the works of Christ (5:36). One of these had just been performed and was public knowledge among the people of Jerusalem.

The third witness is the Father himself (5:37), but the enemies of Christ in their sinful condition were completely out of touch with God and unable to receive his testimony.

The fourth witness is the Holy Scriptures (5:39). To the original hearers of this message the term meant what we now call the Old Testament.

The first verb is probably a declaration rather than a command (the forms are identical in the original language):

> You search the scriptures (ASV); for in them you think you have eternal life: and they are they which testify of me. And you will not come to me, that you might have life (5:39–40).

Constant searching of the Word of God, such as the Jewish religious leaders practiced, does not lead to eternal life unless one accepts the person about whom the Scriptures testify. Life is found not in the Book itself but, through the Book, in the person the Book describes.

The Lord Jesus plainly teaches that the Old Testament foretold his coming, and his answer anticipates all those forms of modern unbelief which deny that Moses wrote the opening books of the Bible: "For had you believed Moses, you would have believed me: for he wrote of me" (5:46).

There is a difference between knowing the facts of the Bible and believing the Bible. Believing the Bible always results in acceptance of Christ.

FEEDING THE FIVE THOUSAND— THE FOURTH SIGN

The feeding of the five thousand is the only miracle performed by the Lord Jesus that is recorded in all four of the Gospels. Actually there were more than five thousand, for the number refers only to the adult men. (For parallel accounts see Matthew 14:13–21; Mark 6:34–44; Luke

9:10–17.) An interesting sidelight is the mention of Philip and Andrew and their apparently close relationship (compare 12:21–22).

The lesson here is that we should surrender all that we have—insignificant as it is—into the hands of the Savior, that he may multiply it for his glory.

The immediate effect of the miracle was that it made the Lord Jesus popular in the wrong way. Many wanted to make him a king (6:15) because he could solve their economic problems, not because they accepted him as Savior and Lord. Hence his abrupt departure "into a mountain himself alone" (6:15).

WALKING ON WATER—THE FIFTH SIGN

Up to this time the Lord Jesus had manifested his glory to his disciples by acts of healing and by providing for material needs. Now by walking on the water, he shows himself to be Lord of creation, superior to all natural laws. "It is I; be not afraid" (6:20). The presence of Christ is all the security anyone will ever need.

SERMON ON THE BREAD OF LIFE—THE FIRST "I AM" SAYING

The unusual events of that day of action were followed the next day by a great sermon and a continuation of the controversy in the synagogue at Capernaum (6:59). As he did so often, the Lord Jesus reasoned from natural needs to spiritual needs, from the things of everyday life to eternal realities. As bread supplies man's physical need, so he himself is the answer to the deeper spiritual need:

And Jesus said to them, "I am the bread of life. He who comes to Me shall never hunger, and he who believes in Me shall never thirst" (6:35 NKJV).

The effrontery of the people was astounding. The day before they had observed the miracle of the loaves and fishes. Now they say, "What miraculous sign then will you give that we may see it and believe you? What will you do?" (6:30 NKJV). Already they were discounting what they had seen, and they began to make unfavorable comparisons with Moses, as if to say, "What you did was nothing compared with what Moses did. Why, he fed a whole nation for forty years in the wilderness with bread from heaven!"

The Lord patiently pointed out to his unreasonable critics that it was God, not Moses, who had given the manna, and that the same God had now sent the true bread from heaven, even Jesus himself. Just as bread will do a starving man no good unless he eats it, so the Lord Jesus cannot save the sinner who refuses him.

THE WORDS OF ETERNAL LIFE

This discourse of the Lord Jesus marked a turning point in his ministry. Some who had been following him now "went back, and walked no more with him" (6:66). They were exposed by the searching judgment of the Lord, "There are some of you that believe not" (6:64).

His plaintive question to the Twelve, "Will you also go away?" evoked an answering question and a ringing affirmation of faith from Peter:

"Lord, to whom shall we go? You have the words of eternal life. Also we have come to believe and know that You are the Christ, the Son of the living God " (6:68–69 NKJV).

42

The true character of Judas Iscariot, known always to the Lord, was revealed here in the Gospel for the first time (6:70–71). The tragedy of the traitor, however, could not dim the light of faith that shone in Peter's confession.

To whom indeed can we go? The Lord Jesus Christ is the answer, the only answer, for us as well as for those original disciples. He alone has "the words of eternal life."

DAILY DEVOTIONAL READINGS

Sunday
John 5:1–14
The helpless healed

Monday
John 5:15–30
Life through the Son

Tuesday
John 5:31–47
Four witnesses to the Son

Wednesday
John 6:1–21
Hunger satisfied—fear dispelled

Thursday
John 6:22–40
The bread of life

Friday
John 6:41–58
Bread from heaven

Saturday
John 6:59–71
The test of discipleship

5

At the Feast of Tabernacles

"And every man went unto his own house. Jesus went unto the Mount of Olives" (7:53; 8:1).

John 7–8

PREPARATION FOR THE FEAST OF TABERNACLES

The opening of chapter 7 shows how the tension had mounted during the ministry of the Lord Jesus. Opposition to him was centered in Judea ("Jewry," 7:1 KJV). His brothers (who are named in Matthew 13:55) had not yet put their faith in him (7:5). They taunted him cruelly about his absence from the religious center of the nation.

In reply, the Lord Jesus did not say that he would not go to Jerusalem at all. He said, "I am not yet going up to this feast, for My time is not yet fully come" (7:8 NKJV).

An interesting sidelight in this Gospel is John's use of the term *Jews* to refer primarily to the religious leaders of the nation (see particularly 7:13).

JESUS ATTENDS THE FEAST

Having come to Jerusalem at his own appointed time, the Lord Jesus began to teach in the temple (7:14). Evidently controversy was still raging about the healing that he had performed on a Sabbath day during his previous visit (7:23). All through the Gospel record the clear implication is that the Lord Jesus had to be a controversial figure. If this is true of ordinary human leaders, how much more so of him. Sides must be chosen. Ultimately we can be only for or against him. Note the widely varying opinions among the troubled populace as described in this chapter.

Near the beginning of his ministry the Lord had spoken of his "hour" which had not yet come (2:4). The thought is repeated here. Underlying the stirring events of this most crucial time in all the world's history was the sovereign purpose of God: "Then they sought to take him: but no man laid hands on him because his hour was not yet come" (7:30).

THE GREAT DAY OF THE FEAST

On the last day of the week-long Feast of Tabernacles, the Lord Jesus gave a triumphant invitation: "If any man thirst, let him come unto me, and drink" (7:37).

Coupled with this invitation was a promise of fullness of life and power through the Holy Spirit (7:38–39).

The reaction of many of the people shows how possible it is to be factually correct without interpreting the facts correctly. They were right in their contention that the Messiah, as prophesied in the Old Testament (Micah 5:2), must

46

come from Bethlehem (7:42). But they completely failed to connect the Lord Jesus with Bethlehem, simply because of his associations with Nazareth in Galilee. Real faith need not be blind; it ought, in fact, to investigate the whole of a situation, not just the appearance.

Nicodemus is seen here for the second time in John. He attempts to apply reason in the case, but his associates are moved by unreasoning hatred. "Out of Galilee arises no prophet," they sneer, conveniently overlooking Jonah, a native of Gathhepher, a town in lower Galilee (2 Kings 14:25). Possibly the enemies of Christ overlooked other Galilean prophets. They certainly overlooked or ignored the great prophecy in Isaiah concerning the Messiah's connections with Galilee (Isaiah 9:1–7). You can find locations mentioned here on the map on page 7.

THE WOMAN TAKEN IN ADULTERY

The twelve verses from 7:53 through 8:11 are not found in some of the oldest manuscripts and are consequently questioned by many Bible students. This is a difficult and exceedingly complicated textual problem, and the evidence for the genuineness of the passage is not clear. While I accept the verses as genuine, I recognize that this is not a question involving doctrinal orthodoxy and would hesitate to base any teaching on this passage alone.

Certainly we are not to understand that the Lord Jesus condoned immorality but that he manifested forgiveness toward the truly repentant. The scribes and the Pharisees who brought the woman to him were not interested in her soul, but only in trapping the Lord Jesus. They proved the insincerity of their motives by bringing the woman alone and ignoring the man involved.

THE LIGHT OF THE WORLD— THE SECOND "I AM"

As the Gospel of Christ is the triumph of eternal life over death, so it is also the triumph of spiritual light over darkness. The second "I AM" saying of the Lord Jesus declares that Jesus is the Light (8:12). This was anticipated in the Prologue, where one of the titles given to the Lord Jesus was the "Light" (1:4–5, 8–9).

THE TWO FATHERS

Every statement of the Lord Jesus provides controversy, because sin cannot abide holiness, or darkness light. Again he is accused of bearing false witness concerning himself (8:13). Again he invokes the Father as a witness, along with himself, to the truthfulness of his claims (8:16, 18).

Coupled with the mention of God the Father is the repeated statement that it was he who sent the Lord Jesus (note, for example, 8:16, 18, 26). A study of the passages in John which refer to the Lord Jesus as the One who was *sent* can be richly rewarding. (Use a concordance.) The Lord Jesus was God's *missionary* to the world. (A Bible dictionary can also be an effective Bible study tool.)

The claims of Christ can be completely baffling to those who do not know him. Notice the questionings and doubts of his hearers:

Where is your Father? (8:19).

Will he kill himself? (8:22).

Who are You? (8:25 NKJV).

They understood not . . . (8:27).

The Lord Jesus promised that the truth would bring freedom. This verse (8:32) is often misapplied by those who are not even interested in the Lord Jesus. The truth spoken of here is the truth concerning Christ himself; to know it is to know him (compare 14:6 and 17:17).

The Jews' reply is pathetically humorous:

> We [are] Abraham's seed, and were never in bondage to any man . . . (8:33).

Had they forgotten the "cruel bondage" (Exodus 6:9) of their ancestors in Egypt? Had they forgotten the Babylonian captivity? How could they ignore the fact that, even as they spoke, they were under Roman domination? Having shown that he referred to a far more terrible slavery than they imagined, the slavery of sin (8:34), the Lord Jesus went on to question their very premise. They were Abraham's *seed*—that was true (8:37). They were natural descendants of Abraham, but they were not Abraham's *children*—(8:39); that is, they did not bear a family resemblance to Abraham, for he never would have rejected the Son of God.

Against their pride of natural descent from Abraham, and their arrogant assumption that God was their Father (8:41), the Lord Jesus interposed the startling comment that their real father was the devil (8:44).

This passage is the answer to those who talk about the universal fatherhood of God. There is a limited sense in which God is the Father of all men in that he is the Creator of all (Acts 17:28). But in the highest and truest sense, God is not the Father of all men. Early in our study we saw the truth that those who believe in the Lord Jesus become children of God (1:12), being born into his family. Since this is so, those who reject Christ are not God's children.

No one except the Lord Jesus had the authority to make such a charge, but let it not be forgotten that he did make it:

"You are of *your* father the devil" (8:44). The first epistle of John, written by the same beloved disciple, develops this teaching (see 1 John 3).

"BEFORE ABRAHAM WAS, I AM"

The virulence of the enemies of Christ was terrible. There seems to be a sneering reference to illegitimate birth (8:41), for no doubt such rumors always dogged his footsteps, and the facts of the virgin birth could not have been made known fully at that time. Later they accused him of being a Samaritan, and a demon-possessed one at that (8:48). Then they asserted, by means of questions, that he was inferior to their "father" Abraham (8:53).

The Lord Jesus in response told them that Abraham rejoiced in his day (8:56). They always twisted his words, but they knew what he meant. He had seen Abraham, for he was—and *is*—the eternal One:

I say to you, before Abraham was, I AM (8:58 NKJV).

At this point they might well have taken up stones to throw at him (8:59), for they had no doubt that he had spoken blasphemous words, and the penalty for blasphemy was death. This was no mere play on words in which the Lord Jesus indulged. This was a deliberate and definite claim to deity. Every Jew would recognize the allusion to the ineffable Name, explained by God to Moses at the burning bush (Exodus 3:14). Not only could he state his eternity in this way—as the I AM—but he was also declaring his Godhood.

This was not the first attempt of the enemies of Christ to put him to death; nor was it the last. But his hour had not yet come (compare 8:20).

DAILY DEVOTIONAL READINGS

Sunday
John 7:1–13
Unbelief—hatred—murmuring

Monday
John 7:14–36
Jesus—sent from God

Tuesday
John 7:37–53
Never man spoke like this man

Wednesday
John 8:1–20
The accusers self-condemned

Thursday
John 8:21–30
The blindness of unbelief

Friday
John 8:31–47
Never in bondage?

Saturday
John 8:48–59
Before Abraham was, I AM

6

Christ the Good Shepherd

> "I am the good shepherd: the good
> shepherd [gives] his life for the
> sheep" (10:11).

John 9–10

HEALING OF THE MAN BORN BLIND—
THE SIXTH SIGN

The disciples' question concerning the cause of the man's
blindness (9:2) shows that they had the same narrow concept
of suffering that Job's friends had in the Old Testament. They
thought of suffering as a punishment for personal sin. Some
suffering is punishment, but certainly not all. While all
suffering can be traced back to Adam's sin (see Romans
5:12), God often has a purpose in suffering that we cannot
fathom (9:30).

The Lord Jesus had previously spoken of himself as the
"light of the world" (8:12). Now he repeats this (9:5) and
illustrates it in the natural realm by healing the blind man.

Why he used the precise method that he did is not clear except that he made an appeal to the man's faith. His obedience indicated his belief that the Lord Jesus could do something for him.

As yet the one-time blind man did not fully know the Lord Jesus. Note the progress of his knowledge and response: at first "A man that is called Jesus" (9:11); then, "He is a prophet" (9:17); later, "of God" (9:33); and finally, "Lord, I believe" (9:38).

By performing this miracle on the Sabbath day (as he had also done in healing the helpless man, John 5), the Lord Jesus sharpened the issue. Again we witness the intense conflict that always must center on the person of Christ in this sinful world—"And there was a division among them" (9:16).

Against the hatred of the religious leaders, the wavering of the crowd, and the temporizing of the parents, the seeing man's testimony is unequivocal and refreshing. He had logic on his side, even though he had no formal training. He had an advantage over the doubters; something had happened to him, and he knew it: "One thing I know, that, whereas I was blind, now I see" (9:25). Note his train of reasoning in John 9:30–33. The only answer that the leaders could give was no answer at all—"They cast him out" (9:34).

The words of the Lord Jesus at the end of the chapter show what a hindrance self-righteousness is. The Pharisees were unaware of any personal need of the Savior; hence, they could not avail themselves of him.

CHRIST THE DOOR AND THE GOOD SHEPHERD—THIRD AND FOURTH "I AM" SAYINGS

The statements made by the Lord Jesus that he is the "door" (10:9) and the "good shepherd" (10:11) intermingle because in the ancient sheepfold the shepherd was literally the door. Stationing himself at the entryway he afforded the sheep both entrance and security.

Christ is not *a* door, but *the* door. Again he voices the exclusive claim:

> I am the door. If anyone enters by Me, he will be saved, and will go in and out and find pasture (10:9 NKJV).

Living in a land where sheep are raised and sacrificed, Jews would appreciate the use of the term *sheep* to describe the people of God. This is a repeated figure in the Old Testament. Probably the most familiar passage in the Old Testament is Psalm 23, known as The Shepherd Psalm. Many other passages use the same sort of expression (note, for example, Psalms 95 and 100).

In the Old Testament, if God's people are sheep, God himself is the Shepherd—"The Lord is my shepherd" (Psalm 23:1). Consequently, the Lord Jesus, speaking deliberately and with a perfect knowledge of all the implications and ramifications of his words, was again claiming to be God when he said, "I am the good shepherd" (10:11). His hearers presumably knew the Old Testament; therefore, he was saying in effect, "Those passages in the Scripture that call God the Shepherd refer to me—I am the One described." This is the conclusion to which the statements come (10:30), fully understood by the Jews (although not accepted by them), as is shown by their now almost automatic response (10:31).

It is impossible to say whether the words concerning the Shepherd were all spoken on one occasion or at two different times. It would seem that all the events of chapters 7–9 occurred during the visit at the Feast of Tabernacles. Possibly the first twenty-one verses of chapter 10 belong also to that visit (see especially 10:21). At least we can be sure that the action starting in verse 22 took place at the Feast of Dedication, which came in December, about two months after Tabernacles. Some would refer everything in chapter 10 to that time.

At any rate, by 10:22 the Lord was less than four months away from the cross. Opposition was rising; hatred was increasing; division was becoming more evident between those who were his "sheep" and those who were not. In spite of all the miracles and all the teaching, the religious leaders still doubted the claims of the Lord Jesus: "How long will you make us to doubt? If you are the Christ, tell us plainly" (10:24).

ONENESS WITH THE FATHER

We have seen that the gospel of John, starting with the Prologue (1:1), emphasizes the deity of the Lord Jesus Christ. In his message after the healing of the helpless man, Jesus claimed self-existence as the Father has self-existence, and announced himself as the Judge of all (5:22, 26–27). In his discourse on himself as the "light of the world," and the consequent debate with the Jews, he appropriated to himself the divine name (8:58).

Here again he strongly asserts his deity: "My sheep hear my voice, and I know them, and they follow me: and I give unto them eternal life; and they shall never perish, neither shall any man [anyone] pluck them out of my hand. My Father, which gave them me, is greater than all; and no man [no one] is able to pluck them out of my Father's hand. I and my Father are one" (10:27–30).

The Scripture teaches that the three persons of the God-head—the Father, the Son, and the Holy Spirit—are one and the self-same God. There is distinction between the persons

("I and my Father"), but unity of the essence or being ("one").

The enemies of the Lord Jesus knew what he was saying. This is clearly explained in the text. When they took up stones to stone him (10:31), as they had done before, with disarming logic and possibly with quiet humor, he asked:

> Many good works have I shown you from My Father. For which of those works do you stone Me? (10:32 NKJV).

Their reply proves that they understood his claim and rejected it and him utterly:

> The Jews answered Him, saying, "For a good work we do not stone You, but for blasphemy, and because You, being a Man, make Yourself God" (10:33 NKJV).

Belief in the Lord Jesus Christ cannot be forced, but unbelief ought to be consistent by acknowledging that Jesus Christ *claimed* to be God (10:33). As has been pointed out in a previous section, much unbelief today masquerades as belief by professing to accept the Lord Jesus as a preeminent teacher and leader, or more subtly still by calling him divine, but redefining the term *divine* to empty it of its real meaning. The issue that the gospel of John raises repeatedly is this: *Is Jesus God?* The book itself answers, "Yes." Does your heart respond, "Yes"?

> But these are written, that you might believe that Jesus is the Christ, the Son of God; and that believing you might have life through his name (20:31).

DOCTRINAL AND DEVOTIONAL APPLICATION

One profitable method of study is to read the cross-references and parallel passages. The book does little to show the harmony of John with the other gospels, for that would enlarge the subject too much for this brief study. This is something you may want to do for yourself.

Another way to compare parallel passages is through topical study. Take, for example, the subject of Christ as the Shepherd, as set forth in John 10. There are also other important passages in the New Testament that speak of Christ in this way. Two passages stand out: Hebrews 13:20–21 and 2 Peter 5:4.

In John 10:11 the Lord Jesus calls himself "the good shepherd." What doctrinal truth is connected with this title? Observe the verse itself: "I am the good shepherd; the good shepherd gives his life for the sheep." Can there be any doubt that the *death* of the Lord Jesus is connected with this title? Certain truths can be gleaned from the passage concerning his death. It was a *voluntary death* (10:17–18). He was willing to die. It was a *vicarious death* (10:11, 15). He was our substitute. It was a *victorious death* (10:18, 28). He conquered sin and Satan.

All of this was still in prospect as the Lord Jesus spoke, but we know now the historical reality of it.

In a similar way you could trace the doctrines connected with each of the other titles (check this for yourself from the Scripture): Just as the Good Shepherd relates to his *death*, so the Great Shepherd relates to his *resurrection*, and the Chief Shepherd relates to his *second coming*. In other words, in these titles we discover the *past, present*, and *future* ministries of our Lord Jesus Christ. As our Great Shepherd, he rose from the dead and is alive to care for us now. As our Chief Shepherd, he is coming again to receive us unto himself and to reward us for faithfulness. We must know him first as the Good Shepherd. That is the basis for all the rest.

DAILY DEVOTIONAL READINGS

Sunday
John 9:1–12
The Light banishes darkness

Monday
John 9:13–25
Experience is the best argument

Tuesday
John 9:26–41
Are we blind also?

Wednesday
John 10:1–10
Only one door!

Thursday
John 10:11–21
The Good Shepherd

Friday
John 10:22–30
Eternally safe

Saturday
John 10:31–42
Son of God—truth or blasphemy?

7

The Resurrection and the Life

"Now a certain man was sick,
named Lazarus, of Bethany, the
town of Mary and her sister
Martha" (11:1).

John 11–12

THE RAISING OF LAZARUS—
THE SEVENTH SIGN

John did not attempt to recount all the miracles of the Lord
Jesus. He refers to many but singles out seven for description. His word for these mighty acts is *signs*, as you may
have noticed in 20:30. (The King James Version sometimes
obscures this by using the word *miracles* for several Greek
words.) We have seen six of the signs in previous chapters.
The seventh one, which conclusively demonstrates the
power of the Son of God, is described in chapter 11. It is the
raising of Lazarus from the dead. Compare the accounts in
the other Gospels of the raising of two other persons: the

daughter of Jairus (Matthew 9:18–26; Mark 5:22–43; Luke 8:41–56) and the son of the widow of Nain (Luke 7:11–17).

An urgent message came to the Lord Jesus from the sisters of Lazarus. But when he received it he "abode two days still in the same place where he was" (11:6). Afterward, when Lazarus was dead (11:14), Jesus started toward Bethany. The disciples manifested some courage, for they had no doubt that danger awaited both the Lord and them as well in Judea (11:8, 16).

The two sisters, Martha and Mary, were both believers in the Lord Jesus, but very different in many respects (see the account of the Lord's visit to their home in Luke 10:38–42). Martha was a woman of action; Mary was more contemplative. Martha "went and met him" (11:20); Mary "sat still in the house" until he summoned her.

THE FIFTH "I AM" SAYING

Martha's words to the Lord Jesus when she met him (11:21) seem to have carried some reproach, as if to say, "Why didn't you come sooner?"

Yet it was in response to her anguished, perhaps bitter, cry that the Lord Jesus gave these wonderful words of assurance:

> "I am the resurrection and the life. He who believes in Me, though he may die, he shall live. And whoever lives and believes in Me shall never die. Do you believe this?" (11:25–26 NKJV).

When Mary came to the Lord Jesus in answer to his call, she said almost the same thing that her sister had said (11:32). In the King James Version the words are the same; but in the original the order is different, giving a different emphasis. Mary's words stressed the personal pronoun—"*my* brother." Mary's utterance was a statement of trust, as though she were saying, "You would have been able to keep him from dying."

There is further indication in the Bible text that this interpretation is correct. The bodily posture of Mary reflects her mental attitude. Mary of Bethany is seen on only three occasions in the gospel records. Significantly, on each of them, she is found at the feet of the Lord Jesus. She "sat at Jesus' feet" (Luke 10:39); she "fell down at his feet" (John 11:32); and she "anointed the feet of Jesus" (John 12:3). She was a true disciple (learner) and a true worshiper.

As always, the Lord supported his words by deeds. Having announced himself as the "resurrection and the life," he proceeded to raise Lazarus from the dead. There is nothing contradictory in his open display of grief (11:35), for he is Son of Man as well as Son of God, and he sorrowed with his friends who sorrowed, even though he knew that Lazarus, almost immediately, would be restored to life. "We have not a high priest which cannot be touched with the feeling of our infirmities" (Hebrews 4:15).

In this miracle God's glory was manifested (11:4, 40) as a sign to those who saw it, that they might believe on the Lord Jesus (11:42).

REACTIONS OF THE JEWS—THE PLOT AGAINST JESUS

The responses of the people were predictable. Some—thank God—believed on him (11:45). But others went to tell the Pharisees, who, along with the leading priests, called a council to plot against the Lord.

Already we have seen several attempts of the crowd to kill Jesus when they were angered at what they supposed to be his blasphemy. This case is different in that it was a carefully laid scheme for getting rid of him. Caiaphas, the high priest, although a contemptible person, by virtue of his office was enabled to speak truly prophetic words from God (11:49–52).

The hour had almost come: "Then from that day forth they took counsel together for to put him to death" (11:53).

Another Passover was approaching, probably the fourth during the Lord's ministry (especially if the feast of 5:1 was a Passover). For more than three years he had walked and taught among the people. "He was in the world, and the world was made by him, and the world knew him not" (1:10). Imagine the suspense in Jerusalem as people everywhere were speculating, "What do you think—that He will not come to the feast?" (11:56 NKJV).

THE SUPPER AT BETHANY

The supper described here (12:1–9) is the same one mentioned in Matthew 26:6–13 and Mark 14:3–9, where additional details are given. Only in John is the woman identified as Mary, the sister of Martha and Lazarus. John had already alluded to the incident in recounting Lazarus' illness (11:2). Mary, by her act of devotion (12:3), showed that she had understood and believed the teaching she had heard at the feet of the Lord. Apparently no one else grasped as accurately as she the truth about his coming death for the sins of the world. The Lord's word concerning her is tender and commendatory: "She has kept this for the day of My burial" (12:7 NKJV). In the parallel accounts he remarks that this act of hers will be told for a memorial of her wherever the gospel is proclaimed.

This passage shows the confusion that results when people are not careful in Bible study. A common error links this scene with the one in Luke 7:37–38, where a woman "which was a sinner" anointed the Lord Jesus' feet. These are two different occasions and two different women. The anointing by the sinful woman was early in Christ's ministry, in the house of a Pharisee called Simon (Luke 7:36, 40); this anointing by Mary in the house of "Simon the leper" (Matthew 26:6) was late in our Lord's ministry, in fact during the last week before his death.

As if this mistaken identification of two different events were not confusing enough, many have increased the confusion by identifying the sinful woman in Luke 7 with Mary Magdalene (Luke 8:2), though there is no connection between them, and further identifying Mary Magdalene with Mary of Bethany!

When Mary performed her act of faith and devotion, the true character of Judas Iscariot, already alluded to by the Lord (6:70–71), was plainly delineated (12:4–6).

CHRIST'S PRESENTATION OF HIMSELF AS KING

The next scene is customarily called the Triumphal Entry. The Scripture presents it as Christ's formal offer of himself to the nation of Israel as their King, as prophesied in the Old Testament (see especially Zechariah 9:9). In order to discover all the details of this striking event, read the parallel accounts in all of the Gospels (Matthew 21:4–9; Mark 11:7–10; Luke 19:35–38).

THE DISCOURSE ON THE "GRAIN OF WHEAT"

The Greeks who approached Philip had a legitimate desire: "Sir, we wish to see Jesus" (12:21 NKJV). The close association of Philip and Andrew has been noticed before (6:7–8).

In contrast to former declarations that his hour had not yet come, the Lord Jesus, anticipating his impending death, now announced, "The hour is come, that the Son of Man should be glorified" (12:23). The great discourse on the "grain of wheat" develops the principle that life and blessing can come only through the Lord's death:

> Unless a grain of wheat falls into the ground and dies, it remains alone; but if it dies, it produces much grain (12:24 NKJV).

The hour for which he had come into the world was now approaching. Christ was soon to be lifted up in death. That 12:32 is a distinct reference to the cross is proved by 12:33.

Still there are doubts and questionings from the crowd. The nation generally is described in these solemn words: "But though he had done so many miracles before them, yet they believed not on him" (12:37). Isaiah's prophecy (KJV, "Esaias") is cited in 12:38–41 concerning the unbelief of the people. Two passages are quoted—Isaiah 53:1 and 6:10. The second quotation is taken from the record of the vision that Isaiah had of the Lord, and John declares that Isaiah saw "his [Christ's] glory" (12:41).

Thus John's account of the public ministry of Christ comes to a close. Tension is high. Belief and unbelief are in deadly combat.

DAILY DEVOTIONAL READINGS

Sunday
John 11:1–16
Faith tested

Monday
John 11:17–31
The resurrection and the life

Tuesday
John 11:32–46
The dead raised

Wednesday
John 11:47–57
One man to die for the people

Thursday
John 12:1–11
Anointed for his burial

Friday
John 12:12–19
Your King comes!

Saturday
John 12:20–50
He came to die . . . to save!

8

In the Upper Room

> "When they heard that Jesus was
> coming to Jerusalem, [they] took
> branches of palm trees, and went
> forth to meet him" (12:12–13).

John 13–14

WASHING THE DISCIPLES' FEET

The gospel of Christ is essentially the victory of life over death and of light over darkness. It is also the triumph of love over hatred and enmity. The love of the Lord Jesus toward his own is seen, not only in the introductory statement of this section (13:1), but also in his actions in the upper room.

The washing of the disciples' feet taught the lesson of humility. This was a task ordinarily done by a servant. By doing this menial task willingly, the Lord Jesus set a pattern for his disciples:

If I then, your Lord and Teacher, have washed your feet, you
also ought to wash one another's feet. For I have given you
an example, that you should do as I have done to you
(13:14–15 NKJV).

This needed lesson in humility and service for others does
not exhaust the meaning of the passage, however, as we see
in the Lord's conversation with Peter. Peter's horrified pro-
test (13:8) brought from the Lord Jesus a statement of the
spiritual significance of his act: "If I do not wash you, you
have no part with Me" (13:8 NKJV).

In response to Peter's impulsive reaction (13:9), the Lord
Jesus drew a contrast that is partially obscured in the King
James Version. The verse more accurately reads:

He who has bathed needs only to wash his feet, but is
completely clean: and you are clean, but not all. For he knew
who would betray him, therefore he said, "not all of you are
clean" (13:10–11).

The bathing, which all except Judas Iscariot had received,
was "the washing of regeneration" (Titus 3:5)—that cleansing, that newness of life, of which the Lord Jesus had spoken
to Nicodemus. That is a once-for-all event. It brings deliverance from the guilt and penalty of sin. There is constant
need, however, for deliverance from the defilement and
power of sin, as represented by the washing of the feet. John
develops this truth of God's cleansing our lives as we confess
our sins to him (see 1 John 1:7–2:2).

BETRAYAL AND DENIAL FORETOLD

The deception of man is evident in Judas Iscariot. In spite of
the fact that the other disciples had lived in close association
with him for three years and had received at least a hint of

his true nature from the Lord Jesus previously (6:70), they apparently suspected nothing. "Who is it?" they inquired.

After the traitor had departed, the Lord Jesus addressed the others as "little children" (13:33) and gave them a "new commandment" (13:34). Love was to be the badge of discipleship by which the true followers of the Lord would be known by those about them.

One might well be disillusioned with human nature after contemplating this scene. Not only was there a traitor among the apostolic band, but even one of those who really believed—and the spokesman of the group at that (6:68)—was solemnly warned by the Lord Jesus that before morning he would deny him (13:38). In contrast to Peter's ardent promises of complete discipleship, he was soon to act the part of a coward and an ingrate.

THE SIXTH "I AM" SAYING—"THE WAY, THE TRUTH, AND THE LIFE"

Is it any wonder that the small company of apostles was plunged in gloom at these words? Perhaps they were thinking: "One of us is a traitor. Apparently we can't trust even Peter. Whom can we trust? Can we even trust ourselves?" The chapter division at this point obscures the connection between 13:38 and 14:1. It is as though the Lord Jesus were answering the terrible bewilderment of their hearts. "Whom can you trust?" He is saying in effect, "Why, you can trust God and you can trust me"; "let not your heart be troubled: you believe in God, believe also in me" (14:1).

It was true that he was going away from them; sadly true also that they had no stability in themselves. But he was not deserting them. The very purpose of his going was for their sakes, with their ultimate welfare in view:

In my Father's house are many mansions [abiding places]:
if *it were* not so, I would have told you. I go to prepare a
place for you. And if I go and prepare a place for you, I will
come again, and receive you unto myself; that where I am,
there you may be also (14:2–3).

This was heartening, and no doubt they sensed it instantly;
but Thomas, vaguely grasping at the hope offered, nevertheless voiced the perplexity of all their minds as he confessed
that he did not really know where the Lord Jesus was going.
And if one does not know the destination, how can one
possibly know the way to get there? (14:5).

Here the Lord Jesus gave to his disciples the truth they
needed so much—the truth we need as well. It is he himself
who is the answer to our questions, the solution to our
problems, the allaying of our anxieties. Not so much what
he has given or what he has said, or even what he has done,
but Christ himself! Jesus answered, "I am the way, the truth,
and the life. No one comes to the Father except through Me"
(14:6 NKJV).

Not the road marker, but the Road; not the truth teacher,
but the Truth; not the life-giver, but the Life. And not *a* way,
but the only Way; not one facet of truth, but *the* Truth; not
one way of life, but Life itself.

Here is further amplification of that which has been
declared from the Prologue on. Christ is the Source of life
(compare 1:4). There is exclusivity about him.

A mistake of human religions is that of thinking that good
parts of many faiths can be combined into one. No, it is
Christ altogether or Christ not at all. His glory he will not
share with another. Those who profess to have fellowship
with God apart from Christ are deceiving themselves.

This is a truth that even some Christians have difficulty
in grasping. Sometimes men are inclined to think, "Well, the

poor heathen worships the true God, because after all there is only one God; therefore, he is but a step from salvation." That step, however, is as wide as the universe. He is not worshiping the true God unless he is worshiping Jesus Christ, for God cannot even be known apart from Jesus Christ. Remember the Prologue again: "No man has seen God at any time; the only begotten Son, which is in the bosom of the Father, he has declared him" (1:18).

Perhaps John was thinking of this statement of the Lord Jesus, this marvelous "I AM" saying, as the Holy Spirit prompted him to write in his first epistle:

> Who is a liar but he who denies that Jesus is the Christ? He is antichrist who denies the Father and the Son. Whoever denies the Son does not have the Father either; he who acknowledges the Son has the Father also. . . . And this is the testimony: that God has given us eternal life, and this life is in His Son. He who has the Son has life; he who does not have the Son of God does not have life (1 John 2:22–23; 5:11–12 NKJV).

Still the disciples did not understand. (We ought not to blame them, for they had more difficulties than we know.) Just one glimpse of the Father, Philip said (as probably all of them thought), will be enough to satisfy (14:8).

If you have not read what has gone before in the Gospel, you might be thunderstruck at the boldness of the Lord Jesus' reply: *He who has seen Me has seen the father* (14:9 NKJV). Therefore, we can say to people; "Do you sincerely want to know what God is like? Then look at Jesus Christ, for he is God."

This One who is indeed God has taken his own into a wonderfully blessed partnership with himself. While here on earth he limited himself by becoming a man and accepting the limitations that are inherent in humanity. Although he always continued to be God, the Lord Jesus lived and worked in only one locality at a time during his earthly ministry. Now he was to leave; he was to be glorified; and through his own he would multiply and magnify his works, just as he had multiplied the loaves and the fishes.

The chief responsibility that we have in this strange but wonderful partnership is *to ask*; his responsibility is *to do* (14:13–14). This does not mean that we are to be passive and to do nothing. Those who are in fellowship with the Lord Jesus will be those most occupied with activity for him. It will be unfrustrated, unvexed activity; seriously urgent yet beautifully and indescribably serene.

Nevertheless, we must not forget that our chief contribution to the heavenly partnership remains simply *to ask*. Contribution? Even that which is our part is a complete dependence upon him. It is he who is working, even in our work. What a blow this is to human pride, a frequent cause of stumbling. There is absolutely no place for pride in this partnership.

THE PROMISE OF "ANOTHER COMFORTER"

In the upper room the Lord Jesus gave the beginning of doctrinal truths that are developed at greater length in the epistles of the New Testament. Luke tells us in his introduction to the book of Acts that his "former treatise" (the Gospel according to Luke) was a record of all that Jesus "began both to do and teach" (Acts 1:1). The implication is that he continued both to do and to teach after his ascension to heaven. Here, in John, in the upper room, is the grand beginning of that teaching concerning the distinctive ministries of the Holy Spirit in this age—teaching that is continued in the epistles.

In the Old Testament and Gospels, the Holy Spirit came upon people and equipped them for special tests and ministries, but he did not permanently live in even the greatest of saints. However, to the disciples, Christ said:

The Spirit of truth . . . dwells with you, and will be in you (14:17 NKJV).

The indwelling was yet future, to become a precious, present reality only after the death and resurrection of the Lord Jesus.

The Holy Spirit was to be "another comforter" (14:16). This, of course, indicated that they had already known one comforter. Here was to be another, just like the first one. Christ himself had been their Comforter (the word means literally "one called alongside," obviously to help). Now he would send to them his other self, so to speak. But while Christ in his unglorified humanity could only be *with* them, the Holy Spirit was to be *in* every one of them and in all of the millions of others who through the age would believe on the Lord Jesus. Here was the motivating power that would enable them to do the "greater works" (14:12).

In 1 John 2:1, where the Lord Jesus is called (in the King James Version) "an advocate with the Father," the word *advocate* is the translation of the same Greek word that is translated *comforter* in this passage. In its Latin form *advocate* means "one called alongside"; it is identical in meaning to the Greek word (which is sometimes written in English as *Paraclete*). So we believers have two advocates, two comforters—one at the right hand of the Father (the Lord Jesus) and one within our very being (the Holy Spirit).

THE NECESSITY FOR PERSONAL APPLICATION

One of the ministries of the Holy Spirit, according to the Lord Jesus, is that of teaching. The apostles later experienced the thrill of his bringing "all things to [their] remembrance" (14:26) as they went about telling of the Lord Jesus, and as some of them were appointed by God to be writers of Holy Scripture. In a more limited, but no less real, way we can know this ministry of the Holy Spirit. It is useless to try to study the Bible without him, for he who is the infallible author is the only completely reliable interpreter. Of course he imparts his teaching to other Christians as well as to us; therefore, we cannot afford to bypass the fund of knowledge that has been built up in the church for all to share.

In the deepest sense, Christ himself is the teacher, and the Holy Spirit is his agent in continuing the ministry of instruction that he began in the upper room. This is brought out more fully in John 16.

Before arising and departing for the garden, the Lord Jesus pronounced his blessing of peace (14:27). He announced also the presence of the "prince of the world," whom he had mentioned before (12:31) and whom he would mention once again (16:11).

What other room on earth ever heard such sayings as were uttered in that room? Though we need not attach importance to mere places, and we dare not erect any shrines, how thankful we can be that the Lord Jesus was willing to grace this sin-cursed earth with his presence and to go in and out of ordinary rooms, bringing with him the glory of his perfect personality. And he will be with us in our houses and our apartments; more than that, in our very lives, if we let him.

DAILY DEVOTIONAL READINGS

Sunday
John 13:1–11
Cleansing from defilement

Monday
John 13:12–17
An example in lowly service

Tuesday
John 13:18–30
The betrayer

Wednesday
John 13:31–35
A new commandment

Thursday
John 13:36–14:12
I AM the Way

Friday
John 14:13–26
Another Comforter

Saturday
John 14:27–3
Blessing of peace

9

F urther Teaching for His Own

> "Every branch in Me that does not bear fruit He takes away; and every branch that bears fruit He prunes, that it may bear more fruit " (15:2 NKJV).

John 15–16

THE SEVENTH "I AM" SAYING— "THE TRUE VINE"

The nation of Israel, although referred to as a vine of God's planting (Psalm 80:8), failed to bring forth fruit for God (Hosea 10:1; compare Isaiah 5:1–7; Matthew 21:33–46). In contrast, Christ is the genuine vine; that is the force of the adjective in the original. The figure for the relationship of believers with the Lord himself is that of a common life that pervades the whole. No figure can express all the truth; here the question of salvation and safe-keeping is not in view. The issue is *abiding* (which has to do with our fellowship with the Lord), and fruit-bearing as the result of abiding.

Three degrees of fruit-bearing are seen: "fruit" (15:2), "more fruit" (also 15:2), "much fruit" (15:5). If there is no fruit whatever the branch is taken away. This perhaps parallels 1 Corinthians 11:30 and 1 John 5:16, where the teaching seems to be that God may bring physical death upon a child of his who dishonors him. Fruit leads to cleansing, for the divine husbandman is not content with the mediocre. He desires "much fruit" (15:8).

Most of us have not yet learned or acknowledged the truth of our Lord's statement, "Without Me you can do nothing" (15:5 NKJV). We are inclined to agree that we cannot do much without him; yet, we have the audacity to think that we can do a little. Only when we come to perfect agreement with him about our total inability do we realize the other side of the picture, which is implied here and stated clearly elsewhere: "I can do all things through Christ who strengthens me" (Philippians 4:13 NKJV).

RESULTS OF ABIDING IN CHRIST

To abide in Christ is to remain in constant fellowship with him. This is the description given in the first epistle of John (see, for example, 1 John 1:3).

In other passages other terms refer to the same state. Here are some examples: yieldedness (Romans 6:13), walking in the Spirit (Galatians 5:16), and being filled with the Spirit (Ephesians 5:18).

One of the results of abiding in Christ is an effective prayer life: "If you abide in Me, and My words abide in you, you shall ask what you desire, and it shall be done unto you" (15:7 NKJV).

Another result is continual joy. What greater joy could come to one than to know that he is loved by the Son of God even as the Son is loved by the Father (15:9)? The grace of the Lord Jesus is displayed in his calling us "friends" (15:15).

His love is constant, but our experience and enjoyment of his love may fluctuate as we fail to abide in him. His desire is that our "joy might be full" (15:11) as we keep his commandments and continue in his love (15:10).

Still another result of abiding, already anticipated in the opening section of the chapter, is continuing fruitfulness:

> You did not choose Me, but I chose you and appointed you that you should go and bear fruit, and that your fruit should remain, that whatever you ask the Father in My name He may give you (15:16 NKJV).

LOVED AND HATED

John's Gospel, as we have seen, is filled with striking antitheses: belief and unbelief, light and darkness, life and death, love and hatred. Having expressed his own deep love for the disciples and having commanded them to love one another (15:12, 17; compare 13:34–35), the Lord Jesus fortifies them against the hatred they will experience from the world.

The word *world* (Greek, *kosmos*) is used in different ways in the Scriptures (there are also other Greek words that are translated "world"). Sometimes it simply refers to mankind generally, as in John 3:16. Sometimes it is the wicked system (the Greek word means "order" or "organization") controlled by Satan, opposed to God, to the Lord Jesus Christ, and to the people of God. The Lord Jesus plainly states that the world hated him (15:18) and that it will hate his followers (15:19).

Considering the Lord's words, it seems strange that Christians sometimes favor the world-system. Like the sinful nature, the world is incorrigibly evil, and believers are not a part of it, although living in the midst of it. What could be more reprehensible than for a creature to hate his Creator? This is the grave charge that the Lord Jesus makes against those who have rejected him. The very fact that he had manifested among men a sinless life increased their guilt: ". . . but now have they both seen and hated both me and my Father. . . . They hated me without a cause" (15:24–25).

Again the Lord Jesus promises the coming of the Comforter, repeating his language of 14:16–17. He indicates that he is telling the disciples these things, the unpleasant as well as the pleasant, that they may be forewarned, that they may not be taken by surprise (16:1, 4). While he was with them, such information was not necessary. But now they must know something of what to expect after his departure.

THE CONVICTING MINISTRY OF THE SPIRIT

Many Bible students have noted that this "upper room discourse" contains the nucleus of much truth that is later developed in the epistles. Teaching concerning the work of the Holy Spirit in the present age indeed finds its core here.

In the providence of God it was expedient for the Lord Jesus to leave his own (16:7). No longer would his presence with them be localized as he fellowshiped with them in bodily form. Now, through the Holy Spirit, his presence would be universal but even more intimate than before, because he would be *within* rather than *beside*.

One of the ministries of the Holy Spirit announced by the Lord Jesus is that of reproving or convicting the world

(16:8). As the gospel is made known to men, only the Holy Spirit of God can incline their hearts to receive it. He convinces men in a threefold way.

First, he convicts of sin, showing that the worst sin, the ultimate sin, is rejection of Jesus Christ (16:9).

Then the Holy Spirit enlightens concerning the righteousness that God requires of man—righteousness that cannot be achieved by man, but can be received only through faith in an unseen Savior (16:10).

Finally, the Holy Spirit shows men the true nature of judgment and reveals to them that Christ has already borne the judgment in their place; for at the cross, Satan, the archenemy, has already been judged (16:11).

This is the third time that the Lord Jesus speaks of the "prince of this world" (12:31 and 14:30). Satan is the real organizer and ruler of the world-system, which hates God and Christ and which will inevitably pour out its hatred upon believers. Paul uses a similar expression for the devil, calling him the "god of this age" (1 Corinthians 4:4, literal translation). We can be thankful that, in spite of this stern truth, God is sovereign, and Satan's power is limited both in degree and in duration.

THE TEACHING MINISTRY OF THE SPIRIT

Now the Lord Jesus amplifies the thought that he had previously expressed concerning the Holy Spirit's bringing all things to the remembrance of the disciples (14:26).

I still have many things to say to you, but you cannot bear them now. However, when He, the Spirit of truth, has come, He will guide you into all truth; for He will not speak on His own authority, but whatever He hears He will speak; and He will tell you things to come (16:12–13 NKJV).

It seems strange at first to hear the Lord Jesus say that he has so much more to tell the disciples after being in intimate and almost unbroken contact with them for more than three years; stranger still to hear him say that they would not be able to take it in even if he told it. However, this is in keeping with the whole tenor of what he has been saying. They are to know a new relationship through the indwelling presence of the Holy Spirit. Now they are to understand things that they could not comprehend even when the perfect teacher, the Lord Jesus himself, explained to them personally.

There was nothing wrong with the Lord Jesus' teaching. The fault lay in the recipients. How could they assimilate all they needed to know of the doctrinal meaning of his atoning death and resurrection when they did not yet even comprehend that those events were so soon to take place? The full understanding could come only after the events, and then only through the interpretation of the Spirit of God himself, who would continue Christ's teaching ministry:

> However, when He, the Spirit of truth, has come, He will guide you into all truth; for He will not speak on His own authority, but whatever He hears He will speak; and He will tell you things to come. He will glorify Me, for He will take of what is Mine and declare it to you (16:13–14 NKJV).

CLOSING DISCUSSION

Earlier in this discourse there were indications that it was not uninterrupted. Some of the disciples had asked questions and interjected comments. This was not a formal oration, but a farewell conversation in which the Lord Jesus naturally talked most, for he had most to say. Here, near the close, the disciples again speak, but first among themselves. Some are perplexed (16:17). The Lord Jesus, graciously responding to their desire to know what he means (16:19), explains to them more fully.

There must be some sorrow in the life of the believer, but it is transitory. Future joy is inevitable (16:22). And there can be joy now through the new relationship in prayer:

> Until now you have asked nothing in My name. Ask, and you will receive, that your joy may be full (16:24 NKJV).

Then as the Lord Jesus spelled it out for them (16:28), they acknowledged that he spoke plainly (16:29–30). Recognizing their faith, he nevertheless sorrowfully foretold the fact that they would soon forsake him (16:32). His reason for telling them these things was that in him they might have peace. Note that he did not promise them, or any of us, peace in the world:

> These things I have spoken to you, that in Me you may have peace. In the world you will have tribulation; but be of good cheer, I have overcome the world (16:33 NKJV).

Peace for anyone is found only in the Lord Jesus Christ, both now and for all eternity.

So closes this most remarkable discourse. Wonderful have been the words of the Lord Jesus as he ministered to men generally; more wonderful still his parting words to his own. Some have compared this section of John that tells of the public ministry of our Lord to the court of the tabernacle in Old Testament times. Following this analogy, the private ministry to his own would correspond to the first room of the tabernacle, the Holy Place. There is yet one more room, the holiest of all—and into that we are about to enter, as we hear what the Lord Jesus says to the Father about us.

DAILY DEVOTIONAL READINGS

Sunday
John 15:1–11
Fruit—more fruit—much fruit

Monday
John 15:12–17
Love one another

Tuesday
John 15:18–27
In the world but not of it

Wednesday
John 16:1–6
Warning of persecution

Thursday
John 16:7–15
The work of the Holy Spirit

Friday
John 16:16–22
Sorrow turned into joy

Saturday
John 16:23–33
Ask . . . receive . . . be of good cheer

10

The Lord's Prayer of Intercession

"When Jesus had spoken these
words, he went forth with his disciples over the brook Cedron, where
there was a garden . . ." (18:1).

John 17

THE TRUE LORD'S PRAYER

The prayer that the Lord Jesus taught his disciples (Matthew
6:9–13) is customarily called the Lord's Prayer. Although
the Lord's Prayer is a pattern given by Christ for his disciples
to follow, it was never prayed by the Lord himself. John 17
records the true Lord's Prayer, offered by him to the Father.

John 17 is sometimes called the "Holy of Holies." This
term may be used in connection with the whole Bible as well
as with the gospel of John. Here God takes us into his

confidence and permits us to hear, as it were, a conversation among the persons of the Godhead concerning us.

THE STRUCTURE OF THE PRAYER

We can outline it thus:

The Lord's Prayer for himself (17:1–5)

The Lord's Prayer for his disciples (17:6–19)

The Lord's Prayer for all believers (17:20–26)

THE COMING OF "THE HOUR"

All of the action of the gospel has been leading up to "the hour" that is mentioned here at the beginning of the prayer (17:1). Early in his ministry the Lord Jesus declared that his hour had not yet come (2:4). A later passage sheds light on the meaning of the "hour":

... and no man laid hands on him; for his hour was not yet come (8:20).

In anticipation of his approaching death, the Lord Jesus announced the arrival of the "hour" at the time when the Greeks asked to see him: "And Jesus answered them, saying, The hour is come, that the Son of man should be glorified" (12:23).

Now, as he contemplates his death on the next day (indeed, according to the Jewish reckoning, on the same day, for the day had begun at sundown), the Lord Jesus speaks these solemn words, "Father, the hour is come" (17:1).

THE LORD'S PRAYER FOR HIMSELF

First of all, the Lord Jesus prayed for himself, not selfishly, but that his work might result in the Father's own glory and the good of all those who believe. The restoration to Christ of the eternal glory that he had shared with the Father (17:5) would indicate that he had accomplished all that he had come into the world to do. The Lord Jesus laid aside his glory for a time, but the Father restored it to him:

> Let this mind be in you, which was also in Christ Jesus: who, being in the form of God, thought it not robbery to be equal with God: but made himself of no reputation, and took upon him the form of a servant, and was made in the likeness of men: and being found in fashion as a man, he humbled himself, and became obedient unto death, even the death of the cross. Wherefore God also [has] highly exalted him, and given him a name which is above every name: that at the name of Jesus every knee should bow, of *things* in heaven, and *things* in earth, and *things* under the earth; and *that* every tongue should confess that Jesus Christ is Lord, to the glory of God the Father (Philippians 2:5–11).

THE GIFT OF ETERNAL LIFE

The Lord Jesus came to give eternal life (3:16). The essence of eternal life is described in these words:

> And this is eternal life, that they may know You, the only true God, and Jesus Christ whom You have sent (17:3 NKJV).

Eternal life is not simply endless existence. Lost men have that as well as the saved. It is a quality of life, the very life of God himself, imparted by his grace to those who believe on the Lord Jesus Christ. Those who know God and his Son Jesus Christ can look forward to eternal life with God.

Although he was not yet on the cross, the Lord Jesus, speaking with the certainty of accomplishment, could say, "I have finished the work which you gave me to do" (17:4). From this vantage point one can see the pattern and get a glimpse at least of the plan which has been carried out step by step, moment by moment, from the beginning in the past eternity (1:1) to the cross—and beyond that to the coming glory of the future eternity (17:5).

HOW THE LORD JESUS ADDRESSES THE FATHER

The Lord Jesus, in his prayer, addresses God in the simplest and most intimate terms. Repeatedly he says, "Father" (17:1, 5, 21, 24). He adds adjectives to this in two places, calling him "Holy Father" (17:11) and "Righteous Father" (17:25). Once he calls him "the only true God" (17:3). Although we are not sons of God in the same sense that the Lord Jesus is the Son of God, we too have the privilege of calling him "our Father" (Matthew 6:9). One who really knows God in this intimate and tender way will be grieved to hear any one appropriating these titles to himself.

HOW THE LORD SPEAKS OF HIS DISCIPLES

In this prayer the Lord Jesus speaks of the disciples as those whom the Father has given him. This thought occurs seven times (17:2, 6 [twice], 11–12, 24).

What an exchange of gifts this is! God has given his Son to the world (3:16). God has given believers to his Son. The Son has given gifts to believers: (1) eternal life (17:2); (2) the Father's words (17:8, 14); and (3) his own glory (17:22).

But we have not given anything; we have only received. There is nothing that we can give until we first become Christ's through the Father's love-gift. Now that we are his, we can give ourselves wholly, willingly, and gratefully to him.

WHAT THE LORD ASKS FOR HIS DISCIPLES

"I pray for them" (17:9). These words of the Lord Jesus are doubly encouraging because they show his continuous intercession for all believers. "He always lives to make intercession for them" (Hebrews 7:25 NKJV; compare Romans 8:34). Christ's first petition for his disciples was that the Father might keep them (17:11, 15). There is a twofold "keeping" in view here.

The first aspect is that of security. Here it is an echo of that strong statement in chapter 10 that no one is able to pluck believers out of Christ's hand or out of the Father's hand (10:28–29).

Christ himself had been keeping them (17:12); now he turns them over, as it were, to the Father. In this keeping role, God is the "Holy Father" (17:11). His holiness demands the eternal safekeeping of those who belong to Christ, because he cannot break his promise.

The mention of Judas—"the son of perdition" (17:12)—is further confirmation of the Lord's previous statement (6:70–71). Judas, while one of the apostolic company, had never belonged to the Lord Jesus, had never really believed on him.

The second aspect of keeping mentioned in the prayer is deliverance and protection from Satan:

I do not pray that You should take them out of the world, but that You should keep them from the evil one (17:15 NKJV).

91

God is able to demonstrate in and through human lives that his children can be victorious in the enemy's own territory, in this world-system controlled and energized by the devil.

Note the repeated mention of the world and of the relationship of believers to it: "the men which you gave me out of the world" (17:6); "in the world" (17:11); "not of the world" (17:14); "not of the world" (17:16); "into the world" (17:18).

What a flood of light these phrases shed upon our responsibility to be ambassadors for Christ in this territory that is now foreign to us! (Compare 2 Corinthians 5:20.)

In addition to safekeeping, the Lord Jesus prays for the sanctification of his disciples (17:17). The Scripture describes this elsewhere as experiential sanctification, a gradual conformity of believers to the image of the Son of God. This will be perfect when he appears to receive us to himself (compare Romans 8:29; 1 John 3:1–3).

In sanctifying us God uses his own pure Word. The psalmist recognized this:

> How can a young man cleanse his way? By taking heed according to Your word. . . . Your word I have hidden in my heart, that I might not sin against You! (Psalm 119:9, 11).

The Lord Jesus had sanctified himself (17:19) in the sense that he had dedicated himself, or set himself apart, to the work of salvation, that the believers might be set apart from sin through the truth of God.

WHAT THE LORD ASKS FOR ALL BELIEVERS

By implication, that which the Lord had been asking for the disciples would apply to all believers. In the closing section of the prayer he makes this plain:

I do not pray for these alone, but also for those who will believe in Me through their word (17:20 NKJV).

Having prayed for the safekeeping and the sanctification of his own, he goes on to pray for their spiritual unity (17:21). Then he prays that they may be brought into his presence to see his glory (17:24).

The unity of believers for which the Lord Jesus prayed is not achieved through the merger of church organizations, especially when important doctrines are ignored for the sake of outward unity.

Christ spoke of an inner unity, effected by the Holy Spirit of God, transcending all external distinctions and worldly barriers. The result of it was to have a powerful impact upon the world—". . . that the world may believe that You have sent Me" (17:21 NKJV); ". . . that the world may know that You have sent Me, and have loved them, as You have loved Me" (17:23 NKJV).

This unity is a reality, for God, by his Holy Spirit, has "baptized into one body" all believers in Christ (1 Corinthians 12:13). The sad fact, however, is that this unity is often unrecognized even by believers themselves. By our actions we often belie our exalted position in Christ!

SHARING HIS GLORY

The divine climax comes in the last petition (17:24). The safekeeping, the sanctification, the unification—all look toward ultimate glorification (compare Romans 8:28–39). The eternal presence of believers in heaven with the Lord is just as certain as if we were already there. He wills it (17:24). Is it conceivable that the prayer of the Son of God could go unanswered? The wonder of it all is overwhelming, but blessedly true!

DAILY DEVOTIONAL READINGS

Sunday
John 17:1–5
Glorify me

Monday
John 17:6–10
I pray for them

Tuesday
John 17:11–16
Keep them

Wednesday
John 17:17–19
Sanctify them

Thursday
John 17:20–21
Unite them

Friday
John 17:22–23
Use them as witnesses

Saturday
John 17:24–26
Let them behold my glory

11

Trial and Crucifixion

"Now in the place where he was crucified there was a garden; and in the
garden a new sepulchre, wherein
was never man yet laid" (19:41).

John 18–19

IN THE GARDEN

The Lord Jesus' agony of prayer in the Garden of Gethse-
mane, which is described in the Synoptic Gospels, is passed
over here (18:1), and the climax of his betrayal and arrest is
rapidly reached. In this record, as he does so often, John
gives us glimpses of Christ's deity:

"Jesus . . . knowing all things that should come upon him,
went forth. . . . As soon then as he had said unto them, I am
he, they went backward, and fell to the ground" (18:4, 6).

He is the one who knows all things and has all power. It
is obvious that his enemies "took Jesus and bound him"

(18:12) only because he permitted them to do so. He was approaching the fulfillment of the words he had spoken earlier:

> No one takes it from Me, but I lay it down of Myself. I have power to lay it down, and I have power to take it again (10:17–18 NKJV).

PETER'S DENIAL

John gives few details of the trial before the Jewish religious leaders Annas and Caiaphas. The appearance before Caiaphas furnished the setting for Peter's denial. The other disciple mentioned in 18:15 was probably John himself. (He never mentions himself by name in the book.) In the garden Peter had been quick to strike out at the enemies of Christ (18:10); later his boldness deserted him and he denied three times that he even knew the Lord (18:17–24, 27), thus fulfilling the words of Christ (13:38) and starkly displaying the frailty of human nature.

CHRIST BEFORE PILATE

As indicated above, John passes over details of the Jewish trial that are given in the Synoptics. The religious leaders had determined beforehand on Jesus' death. However, to maintain the form of legality, they took him before the Roman governor and secured the death sentence from him.

Pilate is portrayed in the Scripture as a cynical, vacillating politician. Though he recognized that the Lord Jesus had done no criminal act (18:38), and though he did not really want to condemn him to death (18:31; 19:6, 12), he finally gave in to the maniacal hatred of the religious leaders against Christ and to their threat to accuse him of disloyalty to the emperor (9:12). He illustrates the truth that weakness in the face of evil is itself evil.

Earlier we saw that John's gospel contains a number of conversations between the Lord Jesus and various individuals. This conversation with Pontius Pilate is one of them. It was a pathetic conversation—not for the Lord, who is the truth, but for Pilate the skeptic, who asked, "What is truth?" (18:38). To be confronted with the truth in the person of the Savior himself, and to evade the truth, is the tragedy of Pilate and of many since his day.

Although there is no indication that Pilate believed in the Lord Jesus, the interview that he had with him made such an impact that he stubbornly insisted on calling Christ the "King of Jews" (18:39; 19:14–15, 19, 22). Perhaps his well-known hatred of and contempt for the Jews had something to do with this. Probably also, being a superstitious man, he was afraid of that which he could not explain in the character of the one who stood before him.

A NOTE ON THE TIME

The Jewish leaders, who had illegally conducted a "trial" of Christ at night, brought him to the Roman governor as early as possible in the morning (18:28). When Pilate delivered Christ to be crucified, it was "about the sixth hour" (19:14). Mark notes that the actual crucifixion at Golgotha began at the "third hour" (Mark 15:25), and all of the Synoptics speak of the darkness that came over the earth from the sixth hour to the ninth hour, at which time the Lord Jesus died.

John was using a system of telling time different from that of the other writers. They used the customary Jewish reckoning, which means that the crucifixion began about nine o'clock in the morning; the darkness came on at noon; and the Lord Jesus died about three o'clock in the afternoon.

John, writing long after the destruction of Jerusalem (which took place in A.D. 70), evidently used the Roman system, which, like ours, began the counting at midnight. If this was the case, then the time mentioned in 19:14 was about six in the morning. This harmonizes with the other accounts.

If John used Roman time in this place, it is likely that he used it throughout his book. What then would be the logical conclusions concerning 1:39 and 4:6?

"CHRIST DIED FOR OUR SINS ACCORDING TO THE SCRIPTURES"

The statement of this topic, taken from 1 Corinthians 15:3, is appropriate here, because John so explicitly shows the fulfilling of Old Testament prophecies. Four times in the passage John calls attention to the fulfilling of specific scriptures (19:24, 27–29, 36–37). The gambling of the soldiers for the seamless robe of Christ had been foretold in Psalm 22:18. (Psalm 22 is often called "The Psalm of the Cross" because it prophesies the death of Christ.)

Realize that it is not the purpose of John's gospel to give a *doctrinal interpretation* of Christ's death. Rather, along with the other gospel records, it furnishes us with the *factual story*. It is the province of the epistles to teach us the meaning of his death. However, as we have gone along through the gospel of John, we have received intimations of the meaning of the cross, certainly enough to accomplish the purpose of the book—that men might believe; and believing, might have eternal life (20:31).

THE LORD JESUS' WORDS FROM THE CROSS

Seven sayings of the Lord Jesus from the cross are recorded in the inspired records.

Three of these are in John. They are probably the third, fifth, and sixth respectively:

1. "Woman, behold your son! . . . behold your mother!" (19:26–27).

Even in his agony, the Lord Jesus made provision for his mother, commending her to the disciple "whom he loved"—undoubtedly John again. Apparently his brothers still did not believe (compare 7:5), and the ties of the new family of God are even stronger than those of Adam's race.

Seven Sayings on the Cross	References
1. Father, forgive them; for they know not what they do	Luke 23:34
2. Today shall you be with me in paradise.	Luke 23:43
3. Woman, behold your son . . . ! Behold your mother!	John 19: 26–27
4. My God, my God, why have you forsaken me?	Matthew 27:46; Mark 15:34
5. I thirst.	John 19:28

6. It is finished.   John 19:30

7. Father, into   Luke 23:46
your hands I
commend my
spirit.

2. "I thirst" (19:28).

The Lord Jesus knew that the prophetic passages of Scripture were being exactly fulfilled. This does not suggest a fabricated fulfillment, but calls our attention to the perfect accuracy of the Word of God. "The Psalm of the Cross" describes the intense thirst brought on by the physical suffering and loss of blood (Psalm 22:14–15).

3. "It is finished" (19:30).

This is a shout of victory, not a cry of resignation nor a moan of despair! Remember that Christ had said to the Father, "I have finished the work which You have given Me to do" (17:4 NKJV). This was not a martyrdom that he endured; it was a work that he accomplished. Here is the meaning of the statement of John the Baptizer, at the very beginning of our Lord's public ministry:

Behold the Lamb of God! (1:36).

John announced that Christ, as the Lamb of God, would take away the sins of the world. On the cross Christ accomplished this.

So the Lord Jesus "gave up his spirit" (19:30 ASV). He had said:

I lay down my life . . . of myself (10:17–18).

"AND THAT HE WAS BURIED"

The Jews were insistent that the bodies of those crucified should not be left hanging on the Sabbath, which began at sundown (19:31). To hasten death they often broke the victim's legs, but it was not necessary to bring on the death of Christ in this cruel manner. He had already dismissed his spirit. John reminds us that this is a fulfillment of Scripture (19:33, 36; compare Psalm 34:20).

However, to make sure that Jesus was already dead, a soldier pierced his side with a spear. John was an eyewitness to this mute testimony of the water and the blood (19:34; compare 1 John 5:6, 8). He undoubtedly thought of this sad scene many times in later life as he had to face heretics who denied the reality of Christ's death.

The entombment is further evidence of his death. This is the reason his burial is included in the facts of the gospel as outlined by Paul in 1 Corinthians 15:1–11. Joseph of Arimathaea, who had been a secret believer (19:38), now came forward, asked Pilate for the body, and tenderly laid it in a new tomb. He was assisted in this by Nicodemus, who appears in the record here for the third and last time (19:39). This apparently was the end of secrecy for these two men—they now openly took their place among the followers of Christ.

That Sabbath was a gloomy day for the disciples (see Luke 24). But it was not the end of the story. A new day was soon to dawn, the first day of the week, the glorious resurrection day.

DAILY DEVOTIONAL READINGS

Sunday
John 18:1–14
Betrayal and arrest of Jesus

Monday
John 18:15–27
Peter's denial

Tuesday
John 18:28–40
Jesus before Pilate

Wednesday
John 19:1–11
Crowned with thorns

Thursday
John 19:12–15
Crucify him!

Friday
John 19:16–30
The cross

Saturday
John 19:31–42
The Scriptures fulfilled

12

Resurrection and Epilogue

"After these things Jesus showed himself again to the disciples at the sea of Tiberias . . ." (21:1).

John 20–21

"HE ROSE AGAIN THE THIRD DAY"

The gospel is incomplete without the resurrection (1 Corinthians 15:3–4). The Lord Jesus said that he had power to lay down his life, and power to take it again (John 10:18). His taking it back again, in resurrection, is the ultimate proof that all his claims were true. Christianity stands or falls on the resurrection of Jesus Christ from the dead. Yes, it stands, because he did rise (compare 1 Corinthians 15:12–20; Romans 10:9).

The resurrection story furnishes a good example of the complementary character of the Gospels one to another. A casual reader might suppose that there were discrepancies, but careful study shows the harmony of the whole.

Needless to say, John does not list all the appearances of the Lord Jesus after his resurrection.

Mary Magdalene (20:1) has been mentioned only once previously in John. She was one of those standing by the cross (19:25). She is identified only briefly in Luke (8:2–3) as one who had been delivered by the Lord Jesus from demon-possession, and as one of the godly women who helped support the ministry of the Lord and his disciples. It was she who discovered the stone rolled away and notified Peter and John (20:2).

The actions of the two men on this occasion seem to be characteristic of them. Peter is the more impulsive; John the more contemplative (20:4–8).

Although the disciples must have been familiar with the Old Testament, and although the Lord Jesus on several occasions had foretold not only his death but also his resurrection, they still did not understand! Only illumination by the Spirit of God could make the truth real to them:

> For as yet they knew not the scripture, that he must rise again from the dead (20:9).

THE LORD JESUS APPEARS TO MARY MAGDALENE

The appearance of the risen Lord to Mary Magdalene is poignant. The weeping, bewildered woman is still looking for the body of Jesus. In her grief she pleads with the one whom she supposes to be the gardener to tell her where his body is (20:15). In speaking her name the Lord Jesus makes himself known. Who can describe the tenderness of that word and the still deep, but now joyful, bewilderment of her reply? It is one of the excellencies of the Word of God that it does not try to describe such things; rather it presents them directly to the believing heart so that they can be sensed in a more profound manner than mere description can convey.

What is the meaning of the Lord's words, "Touch me not . . ." (20:17)? Some, on the basis of Matthew 28:9, have supposed that the Lord, between this appearance to Mary and the appearance to the group of women, ascended to heaven and came back again. There is no real evidence in the Scripture for this view of a private ascension before the one described as taking place forty days after the resurrection (Acts 1:9). Actually the form of expression in the original (John 20:17) indicates that Mary was touching him, in fact was holding on to him just as the other women are described as doing in Matthew. The idea is that she was to stop holding on to Christ, for there was much to be done before his ascension to the Father. As the risen Lord, he had entered into a new relationship with his own. Mary had the great responsibility of informing the disciples of his resurrection, and he had much to teach them before he ascended (compare Acts 1:3). The present tense verb "I ascend" is used in a futuristic sense.

APPEARANCE TO THE APOSTLES—
THOMAS ABSENT

John's mention of the "same day at evening" (20:19) seems to corroborate the view that he uses Roman reckoning of time, because in the Jewish reckoning evening would mark the beginning of a new day. Note the continuing fear of the disciples. They were meeting together secretly (20:19), not knowing what would be the outcome for them personally.

Some unbelieving critics of the Bible have theorized that the disciples were so eager for Jesus to rise from the dead that they convinced themselves, and others, that he had done so. How different were the facts! These men were not gullible. They were hard-headed and difficult to convince. We can partially imagine their feelings if we try to put ourselves in their situation. Suppose you had seen a loved one die, had watched his burial, and then on the third day he had come into your room (without opening the door) and had talked with you. Would you not have mental and emotional problems? Let us not be too hard on the disciples. Let us remember that they did not yet have the teaching ministry of the Holy Spirit which the Lord Jesus had promised them.

Just as the Lord had calmed the troubled sea, so he calmed and can calm troubled hearts—"Peace be unto you" (20:19, 21). His breathing on them, and his words about receiving the Holy Spirit (20:22), are probably anticipatory of the great event of Pentecost which was soon to follow (Acts 2:1). There need be no problem about these words:

> If you forgive the sins of any, they are forgiven them; if you retain the sins of any, they are retained (20:23 NKJV).

The disciples themselves did not have any power to forgive sins, but in preaching the gospel they were agents for God. In declaring that God forgives all who believe on his Son and does not forgive those who do not believe, they fulfilled the function described here by the Lord.

The ministry of the gospel is, as Paul declares, "the savor of death unto death" as well as "life unto life" (2 Corinthians 2:16).

APPEARANCE TO THE APOSTLES— THOMAS PRESENT

Thomas was a man hard to convince, a man who had to be shown (20:25), which makes his subsequent testimony all the more valuable. The next appearance that John describes was a week later (this is the likely meaning of "after eight days" in 20:26). This time Thomas was present, and the Lord Jesus gave him the opportunity to do just what he had said would be necessary to convince him (20:25, 27). It would seem that this was unnecessary. The appearance of the Lord Jesus was enough for Thomas, not only to acknowledge that it was really Christ risen from the dead, but also to worship him, owning him as Lord and God (20:28).

Thomas' confession of faith and the Lord Jesus' reply introduced the statement of the purpose of the book, which has been noticed a number of times throughout our study. Note the connection:

> Blessed are those who have not seen and yet have believed. And truly Jesus did many other signs in the presence of His disciples, which are not written in this book; but these are written that you may believe that Jesus is the Christ, the Son of God, and that believing you may have life in His name. (20:29–31 NKJV).

We are among those who have not seen. It was for us, and for others like us, that the book was written. Life through believing on the Lord Jesus Christ! May your response be like that of Thomas.

EPILOGUE—AT THE SEA OF TIBERIAS

The "Sea of Tiberias" (21:1) is another name for the Sea of Galilee. It was a familiar fishing spot for the men who were together on this occasion. John was there, for he was one of the "sons of Zebedee" (21:2). Although the Lord Jesus had appeared to them twice, as described in the preceding chapter (compare 21:14), the disciples did not know what they were to do. What could be more natural than that Peter and the others should return to the occupation they had before the Lord called them (Luke 5:1–11)?

On that former occasion the Lord gave them a miraculous catch of fish as a prelude to his command that they were to follow him and become fishers of men. Now he teaches them the lesson all over again under new conditions. He shows them that apart from him they cannot even be successful fishermen (21:3). When they follow his direction the result is more than satisfactory (21:6).

This is a memorable scene; yet again the use of description is sparse. Here is the Lord Jesus standing on the shore in the early morning, at first unrecognized. The disciples in their fishing boat are about a hundred yards out ("two hundred cubits," 21:8). John, with his characteristic spiritual discernment, is the first to say, "It is the Lord" (21:7). Peter, with his characteristic love of action, is the first to do something. He plunges into the lake and hastens to his Savior.

PETER IS RECLAIMED

At this unusual breakfast on the shore of the Sea of Tiberias the Lord Jesus conducts the last interview in the book—this time with Simon Peter. John has not said anything about Peter's grief after his denial of the Lord, but Luke indicates that it was deep and real (Luke 22:62). Although the Lord Jesus had appeared to Peter before this (Luke 24:34; 1 Corinthians 15:5), this is their first recorded conversation since that sad night when Peter had said three times that he did not know Christ and had no connection with him.

Possibly the Lord Jesus drew Peter apart from the group to ask him the all-important question, "Do you love me?" (21:15–17).

Many commentators have drawn dogmatic inferences—often contradictory to one another—from the fact that two different Greek words for love are used in the passage. The Lord uses one word; Peter answers with another. The Lord uses his same word; Peter answers with his same word. Then the Lord uses Peter's word, and Peter answers with it. In my opinion, it is doubtful that any distinction can be pressed here.

The main point is that the Lord Jesus was graciously giving Peter opportunity to reaffirm his love three times after his threefold denial. By commissioning Peter to feed his lambs and his sheep, the Lord Jesus shows that he has completely forgiven Peter.

Again we read the familiar words, "Follow me" (21:19), as at the beginning (compare Luke 5:10 with Matthew 4:18–19 and Mark 1:16–17). Peter, like most of us, wants to know about another man's responsibility: "What *shall* this man do?" (21:21 NKJV). The Lord Jesus makes it clear that each disciple has an individual responsibility to his Lord regardless of what the Lord's will is for others—"You follow me"—the *you* is emphatic.

This other man is John, who wrote the book, and his authorship is attested evidently by a group of Christians at the time of writing (21:24).

"If I will . . ." (21:21, 23). The Lord Jesus Christ—the eternal Word made flesh, the worker of the mighty signs, the speaker of the "I AM" sayings, the crucified one, risen gloriously from the dead—is the sovereign master of our lives. May this be blessedly true in your experience.

DAILY DEVOTIONAL READINGS

Sunday
John 20:1–10
The empty tomb

Monday
John 20:11–23
From fear to joy

Tuesday
John 20:24–29
My Lord and my God!

Wednesday
John 20:30–31
Why John wrote this gospel

Thursday
John 21:1–14
From failure to fruitfulness

Friday
John 21:15–19
Do you love me?

Saturday
John 21:20–25
Follow me

Bibliography

The following books are recommended to help you in further study of the gospel according to John.

Boice, J. M. *The Gospel of John: An Expositional Commentary.* Grand Rapids, Mich.: Zondervan Publishing House, 1985. *An extensive verse-by-verse study with numerous personal and contemporary illustrations.*

Harrison, E. F. *John the Gospel of Faith.* Everyman's Bible Commentary. Chicago: Moody Press, 1967. *A basic, simplified, verse-by-verse study.*

Hendricksen, Wm. *Exposition of the Gospel of John.* New Testament Commentary.Grand Rapids, Mich.: Baker Book House, 1961. *Thorough and readable. Verse-by-verse treatment with concise summaries of each section.*

Macaulay, J. C. *Devotional Commentary on the Gospel of John.* Grand Rapids, Mich.: Wm. B. Eerdmans, 1941. *Studies with spiritual insight and practical application.*

Morgan, G. C. *The Gospel According to John.* Vol. IV of Studies of the Four Gospels. New York: Fleming H. Revell, n.d. *Rich expositional work.*

Bibliography

Ryle, John Charles. *Expository Thoughts on the Gospels.* 3 vols. on John. Greenwood, S.C.: Attic Press, 1969. *A new edition of an earlier edition of the work published by Zondervan. Rich verse-by-verse devotional commentary.*

Tasker, R. V. G. *The Gospel According to John.* Tyndale New Testament Commentary. Grand Rapids, Mich.: Wm. B. Eerdmans Publishing Co., 1960.

Tenney, M. C. *John, the Gospel of Belief.* Grand Rapids, Michigan: Wm. B. Eerdmans, 1948, 1973. *An analytical study. The Gospel is unfolded by analysis of each paragraph. Excellent outline.*

Westcott, B. F. *Commentary on the Gospel According to St. John.* Grand Rapids, Mich.: Wm. B. Eerdmans, 1950. A minute analysis, verse-by-verse. Thorough introduction. Indispensable for serious study of John.